Women
Responding
to the Spirit

Women Responding to the Spirit

Selections from the Madeleva Lectures

Edited by Jessica Coblentz
and Daniel P. Horan

Paulist Press
New York / Mahwah, NJ

Cover image by Pawel Czerwinski / Unsplash.com
Cover design by Sharyn Banks
Book design by Lynn Else

Library of Congress Cataloging-in-Publication Data
Names: Coblentz, Jessica, editor. | Horan, Daniel P., editor.
Title: Women responding to the spirit: selections from the madeleva lectures / edited by Jessica Coblentz and Daniel P. Horan.
Description: New York, Mahwah, NJ: Paulist Press, [2025] | Includes bibliographical references. | Summary: "A compilation of excerpts from the Madeleva Lectures"—Provided by publisher.
Identifiers: LCCN 2024036537 (print) | LCCN 2024036538 (ebook) | ISBN 9780809157426 (paperback) | ISBN 9780809188543 (ebook)
Subjects: LCSH: Women—Religious aspects—Catholic Church.
Classification: LCC BX2347.8.W6 W653 2025 (print) | LCC BX2347.8.W6 (ebook) | DDC 282.082—dc23/eng/20241024
LC record available at https://lccn.loc.gov/2024036537
LC ebook record available at https://lccn.loc.gov/2024036538

ISBN 978-0-8091-5742-6 (paperback)
ISBN 978-0-8091-8854-3 (ebook)

Published by Paulist Press
997 Macarthur Boulevard
Mahwah, NJ 07430
www.paulistpress.com

Printed and bound in the
United States of America

For our students at Saint Mary's College.
May you come to know and to realize
your own potential for greatness.

Contents

Preface

A Woman Seeking "More"

In 1994 during the sesquicentennial of Saint Mary's College in Notre Dame, Indiana, Gail Porter Mandell offered a lecture, "Madeleva: One Woman's Life," in the college's esteemed annual lecture series, the Madeleva Lecture in Spirituality. In it, Mandell recounted the relatively unremarkable origins of Eva Wolff, the woman who would grow up to become an acclaimed poet, influential figure in American religious life, respected educator and administrator, and the namesake for that very lecture series: She became Sister Madeleva Wolff, CSC.

"Madeleva was born on May 24, 1887, to August and Lucy Arntz Wolff," explained Mandell. "They named her Mary Evaline, but called her 'Eva' or 'Sis.' She was the second child of four (the last boy died soon after birth), and the only daughter. Some of her earliest memories were of playing in her father's harness shop with her brothers, Fred and Vern. She loved the outdoors, especially the lake that surrounded the island city of Cumberland. She swam all summer and was the first on skates every winter, with the 'ice cracking under every stroke.'"[1] Eva grew up in this modest Wisconsin city until 1905, when the Wolff family's commitment to education led her to follow her older brother, Fred, to the University of Wisconsin in Madison, where the young woman embraced her studies and the rich extracurricular life of the university and its surrounding city.[2]

Of this first year in Madison, Mandell recounts that Sr. Madeleva "was happy enough with her studies and did well, but something was missing. As she told the story later, one night after a party she sat brushing her long hair in her room in the boarding house where she lived....The thought suddenly came to her, 'There must be more to life than this.'"[3] Her search for something "more" would bring Eva to Saint Mary's College: "Although Eva had never heard of Saint Mary's before," explains Mandell, "she had decided to apply after seeing an advertisement in a magazine."[4] Eva transferred there in 1906 at the age of nineteen.

At Saint Mary's, Eva discovered a passion for poetry, and after her junior year, she entered religious life with the college's sponsoring congregation, the Sisters of the Holy Cross. Eventually, this community would bestow upon her a new name—Madeleva. "The name chosen for her by her superiors pleased her; she interpreted it as 'a combination of the names of the mother of God, Magdalen, the friend of Christ, and Eve, the mother of mankind.' Here was the full spectrum of feminine experience to identify with. She saw her new life as a religious not as closing off but as opening up possibilities for self-development and self-discovery."[5]

Recognizing Sr. Madeleva's intellectual promise, the congregation went on to support her PhD studies in English at the University of California, Berkeley, where, in 1925, she was "the first sister and one of very few women...to complete requirements for the doctoral degree."[6] She would become a well-published and sought-after poet in the decades that followed.[7] The congregation also called Sr. Madeleva to leadership as an administrator in more than one of its educational institutions, including Saint Mary's College, where she would become its long-serving and most famous president. All the while, Sr. Madeleva became a friend and regular correspondent of some of the twentieth century's most influential minds in and beyond the Catholic Church.

"Reading her obituary in the *New York Times*, who would have thought that one woman could attain success in so many different ways—as a poet, a scholar, an educator, and an administrator—any one of which ordinarily requires an entire lifetime?" wonders Mandell. "How did 'the most renowned nun in the world,' as one columnist called her at the time of her death, evolve from such unlikely beginnings?"[8] When Sr. Madeleva transferred to Saint Mary's, a decision that appeared a singular, if not bold, choice to pursue "more," she could not have imagined it would be the catalyst for this truly remarkable life. In retrospect, it is an early and discreet moment in a life that was defined by this kind of faithful striving. Over and over again, Sr. Madeleva's pursuit of "more" for herself and for others resulted in something beyond what she herself could have initially conjured.

As in Sr. Madeleva's personal life, her professional life was marked by modest hopes that regularly led her into new, unpredictable enterprises, many of which became projects of great consequence. For example, recounts Mandell, "In the early 1940s, women, including religious women, as well as laymen were barred from the graduate study of theology by all Catholic universities in the United States, in spite of a shortage of teachers. In 1942, the National Catholic Education Association [NCEA] identified this shortage as one of the biggest problems facing Catholic education, and appointed Sr. Madeleva to explore possible solutions. Every graduate school she approached, including Catholic University, refused to consider setting up a program for sisters and laypeople. No alternatives seemed to remain." Wanting more for women religious and their lay counterparts in Catholic education and ministry, Sr. Madeleva took on another unforeseen venture. "At the next meeting of the NCEA, Sr. Madeleva amazed herself by announcing to the group: 'I do not know how we will do it, but this summer we will offer at Saint Mary's a six-weeks' graduate program in Theology.'"[9]

Sure enough, "by the centennial of the college in 1944, the School of Sacred Theology was organized and running. Eighteen sisters registered in the summer of 1943."[10] Having set out to provide women religious with the training that, in Sr. Madeleva's mind, was simply necessary and deserved, the School of Sacred Theology would go on to change the course of Catholic theology in the twentieth century and beyond. Today it is frequently cited as the United States' first fulltime doctoral program in Catholic theology to admit laypeople. "By the time the School closed almost twenty-five years later, Saint Mary's had granted 76 doctoral and 354 master's degrees in theology to sisters as well as laymen and laywomen"—among them, notable scholars such as Sr. Margaret Brennan, IHM and

Mary Daly.[11] The Madeleva Lecture that honors the woman who as president inaugurated this pathbreaking graduate program is likewise a venture that has exceeded what many could have anticipated at its origins.

THE HISTORY OF THE MADELEVA LECTURE

In March of 1984, Dr. Keith Egan, the renowned scholar of Carmelite spirituality and the chairperson of the Saint Mary's College religious studies department, submitted a proposal to the Board of Trustees for an academic center that would focus on spirituality. One of the first of its kind, the then-titled Center for Spirituality (today called the Center for the Study of Spirituality) was a distinctive and ambitious enterprise. According to Egan, the Center would bring together two of the greatest legacies of Saint Mary's: its identity as a Catholic women's college and the significant tradition of Sr. Madeleva's School of Sacred Theology. As he stated in the original proposal document, "The proposed Center will foster the acquisition of the skills for reflection upon religious experience, the kind of reflection that was characteristic of Saint Mary's pioneering Graduate School of Theology from the 1940s through the 1960s. The Center will continue this spirit in a new way that corresponds to the needs of our times."[12]

The idea for this Center dates to the spring of 1983 when Egan was still a faculty member at Marquette University and was recruited to the Saint Mary's religious studies department. Egan recalled that during his on-campus interviews with Dr. William Hickey, the vice president for academic affairs, and Dr. John Duggan, the president of the college, he floated the idea of such a Center and was pleasantly surprised at their supportive response. President Duggan felt that such an initiative was very much in keeping with the college's traditions and mission.[13] When Egan moved to South Bend in fall 1983 to assume his new position as a faculty member and chair of the department, he began drafting a formal proposal to submit to the Board of Regents for approval. Still supportive of the idea, President Duggan invited Egan to deliver his pitch to the board on

March 23, 1984. According to Egan, the discussion that followed lasted not much more than "ten or fifteen minutes" before the board enthusiastically approved the request to establish a "Center for Spirituality."[14] In addition to the governing board's support, within months of the approval, the Sisters of the Holy Cross—the sponsoring congregation of Saint Mary's College—pledged a lead gift of $100,000 to fund the Center after a request for financial support from President Duggan to Superior General Sister Olivia Marie Hutcheson, CSC.[15]

The founding vision for the Center included several initiatives, events, workshops, and conferences that would foster appreciation for and engagement with a range of spiritual practices, as well as the then newly emerging field of the academic study of spirituality. Emphasis was always to be placed on the role of women in theology, society, and the Church, with particular attention given to ways the Center could support and foster the work of women scholars in the field. Among the proposed list of possible programs was the establishment of an annual lecture. In fact, it was the first potential program on the list! The original description read:

> The Center will sponsor an Annual Lecture [to be known as "The Madeleva Lecture" or another appropriate name, e.g., to be named in honor of a sponsor who would underwrite this lecture series] on a theme concerning Christian Spirituality especially as this theme relates to Women in the Church. The lecturer will be asked to submit in advance a text that can be published in book form. The series of published lectures will constitute a permanent contribution by Saint Mary's College to the development of the Spirituality of Women in America.[16]

The original idea was to have the proceeds of the sale of the published lecture, which would be made available at the time of the live presentation, help fund the Center's initiatives. And for many years that was the case. Over time, that model became less tenable, but the tradition of publishing the annual Madeleva Lectures continued and continues to this day. From the first lecture in spring 1985 through today, the same publisher has remained a partner with the Center. Egan recalled the enthusiasm of Rev. Kevin Lynch, CSP, the then-publisher of Paulist Press, in signing on to this plan.

When asked about how the lecture came to be named after Sr. Madeleva, Egan shared that it came to him shortly after returning to Milwaukee after interviewing for the Saint Mary's position in 1983. In addition to the legacy Sr. Madeleva left to Catholic theology after founding the graduate school, Egan also had a personal experience of Sr. Madeleva decades earlier in the late 1950s that had stayed with him. As he tells the story, he was a young Carmelite friar at the time, serving as an assistant principal of Joliet Catholic High School in Joliet, Illinois. Egan had the idea of inviting Sr. Madeleva to the school in the fall of 1957 or 1958 to give a talk. He recalled that "the invitation was extended to Sr. Madeleva because of her preeminence and leadership in American Catholic education especially the education of women."[17] After her presentation, Sr. Madeleva asked Egan to drive her around the city of Joliet so that she could make some fundraising visits to local alumnae of Saint Mary's. As Egan put it, he did some "chauffeuring for Sr. Madeleva" and got to know her a little bit, which left a lasting impression. Afterward, she gifted him with an autographed copy of her memoir, *My First Seventy Years*.[18] In many ways, to name the lecture after Sr. Madeleva was an obvious choice and one that received full support from the Saint Mary's administration.

The planning of the first annual Madeleva Lecture began shortly after the formal approval for the establishment of the Center. Egan knew that it was important to have an influential and well-known woman theologian be the inaugural Madeleva lecturer if the series was to carry the gravitas and import hoped for it. Four decades later, Egan recalled that the choice for the first lecturer was never a question for him. It would be Dr. Monika Hellwig (1929–2005), who was then a professor of theology at Georgetown University and would later serve as the President and Executive Director of the Association of Catholic Colleges and Universities in Washington, DC. Egan recounted that Hellwig was not only an excellent theologian, but she was also one of the best-known Catholic women theologians in the country at that time.[19] As her *Washington Post* obituary explained in 2005, she was "a former nun who attended the Second Vatican Council, [and] was respected by laity, theologians and church leaders even when she publicly expressed differences of opinion with church hierarchy."[20]

Hellwig accepted Egan's invitation to deliver the inaugural Madeleva Lecture in the spring semester of 1985. Her lecture, titled "Christian Women in a Troubled World," opened with this memorable line, which launched this important series and tied it back to its namesake's legacy: "The series here initiated is dedicated to a great woman, Sister Madeleva of the Congregation of the Holy Cross, and it is the intent of all that is done in her name that other Christian women should come to know and to realize their own potential for greatness."[21] Like Sr. Madeleva, Hellwig was herself a great woman and a true advocate for women in theology. Her own biography, which includes being born in Europe and fleeing the Nazi regime in Germany as a child, entering a Catholic religious community where she served the poor and studied academic theology, and graduating with her doctorate from the Catholic University of America in 1966, informed her commitment to bridging the everyday experiences of real people with the insights and inspiration of academic theological reflection. Her stature and vision aligned well with Egan's dream of an annual lecture series that would feature women scholars of religion contributing to a growing body of work in Christian spirituality. In the years and decades that followed, the Madeleva Lecture series has continued this tradition.

OVERVIEW OF THE BOOK

The idea for a project like this present book, which would collect selections of the annual Madeleva Lectures into one accessible volume, had been circulating for several years. Keith Egan had long advocated for ways to share with a broader audience the wisdom and insight contained in these dozens of published lectures. While discussed by Egan and the team at Paulist Press long ago, various circumstances, personnel changes, and other challenges prevented the commencement of the editorial planning and work to make this idea a reality. Fast forward to 2021 when the Center's new director, Dr. Daniel P. Horan, and members of the team at Paulist Press, now led by editorial director Paul McMahon, met to discuss ways to help elevate and promote this formidable lecture series. At that meeting, McMahon presented the idea of a one-volume compendium of Madeleva Lecture excerpts, and Horan immediately agreed that it was a great idea. Shortly thereafter, Horan enlisted his colleague Dr. Jessica Coblentz to serve as coeditor of the project. And our work was underway.

Given the scope of the project, the array of themes, the range of distinctive voices, and the deadline we proposed—with hopes that this volume would be available during the fortieth-anniversary year of the founding of the Center—required a strategy for reviewing and editing the sheer volume of content. We made an editorial decision that we would only consider for inclusion those lectures whose volumes were already in print, meaning that the last lecture included in this volume is Dr. Nancy Pineda-Madrid's 2019 Lecture, "Theologizing in an Insurgent Key: Violence, Women, Salvation," which was published in book form in early 2022.[22] Because of several years when the lecture format shifted away from a solo lecturer (such as in 2005, when a panel of previous lecturers were invited to speak about Vatican II or 2015, when a panel of millennial-generation women discussed their hopes for the Church), there were a total of thirty-three published Madeleva Lectures to review. We decided early on that Dr. Gail Porter Mandell's 1994 lecture on the life of Sr. Madeleva would be better incorporated into this introduction. This left thirty-two volumes to examine.

Early in the editorial planning process, we brainstormed with McMahon about what format would best shape a project like this. How long should the book be? Would we include something from every lecture from 1985 to 2019? Should the passages be long or short, self-contained wholes or perhaps small "inspirational" quotations? How would the selections be organized? Should we begin with specific categories and match the volumes to particular headings? Or should we enlist a more inductive editorial approach, which would limit predetermination and allow the spirit of the texts to inspire the structure?

We decided that we preferred an inductive approach, which led us to read the entirety of all thirty-two texts, noting passages along the way that might lend themselves to be excerpted. After separately reading through the volumes, we would meet to compare notes and then agree upon selections to excerpt. With so much meaningful content to sort through, we were pleasantly surprised to find that we were often in agreement and noted that an organic set of five themes emerged according to which we could organize the volume's chapters. After spending so much time with these texts, we felt that it was best to let the words of the lecturers speak for themselves without any additional commentary or introductions from us. We did create titles for each of the passages and wanted to include both the lecturer's name and the date of the lecture. We also organized the excerpts of the chapters in chronological order.

Each of the volume's five chapters contains excerpts from past Madeleva Lectures according to a particular theme. Chapter 1 focuses on excerpts from lectures that attend to the themes of "Prayer and Spirituality." This includes reflections from Monika Hellwig's inaugural Madeleva Lecture, as well as the lectures of Mary Collins, OSB; Maria Harris; Mary Boys, SNJM; and Kathleen Norris.

Chapter 2 collects reflections on "The Church," especially the place in and role of women in the Church. Lecturers in this section include Denise Lardner Carmody; M. Catherine Hilkert, OP; Mary Ann Hinsdale, IHM; Kathleen Hughes, RSCJ; and Catherine Clifford.

Chapter 3 examines "Holy Women" in the tradition, which includes both those canonized saints as well as other exemplars of Christian life. The contributors included in this chapter are Dolores Leckey; Jeannette Rodriguez; M. Shawn Copeland; Anne E. Patrick, SNJM; and Wendy M. Wright.

Chapter 4 gathers together excerpts from lectures that focus on themes in "Gender and Sexuality." The authors of these reflections include Sandra M. Schneiders, IHM; Elizabeth Dreyer; Joan Chittister, OSB; Lisa Sowle Cahill; Diana Hayes; Sidney Callahan; Mercy Amba Oduyoye; and Nancy Pineda-Madrid.

And chapter 5 explores themes related to "Culture and Dialogue." The contributors in this section include Elizabeth A. Johnson, CSJ;

Margaret Farley, RSM; Susan A. Ross; Barbara Fiand, SNDdeN; Kwok Pui-Lan; Christine Firer Hinze; Marianne Farina, CSC; and Ilia Delio, OSF.

Readers will note that some selections could be presented in more than one of these thematic chapters. While reading, some may also note additional themes that could have served to organize its chapters. Creativity and imagination were among some of the other recurrent themes that stuck out to us, for instance. With our authors addressing so many important themes in theology, spirituality, and the life of women, no singular framework could capture them. Readers may also wonder why we opted to feature one selection of an author's lecture but not some other part. After all, the selections of this book are but a glimpse of the insight and wisdom on offer in the Madeleva Lectures. It has always been our hope that the passages featured here will inspire readers to pick up and read the lectures in their entirety—whether again or for the first time.

In addition to the five chapters of lecture excerpts, we have included two appendices: the text of the "Madeleva Manifesto" as well as a list of all the Madeleva lecturers that had already been delivered at the time of this publication. Drafted by fifteen former Madeleva lecturers in 2000, the Manifesto offers "a message of hope and courage to women of the church," especially to "the young women of the church," who are the Church and will be its future. We offer this book in the same spirit as the Manifesto. Though it showcases the wisdom of past Madeleva Lectures, we believe the words of our authors can continue to serve as inspiration for the present and especially for the future.

Chapter I

Prayer and Spirituality

A USABLE PAST FOR AN IMPOSSIBLE FUTURE

Monika Hellwig (1985)

From all of this there emerges the important question as to how we are to discern or identify the "usable past" that provides us with models, with insights, with warnings, with hope and challenge. Concerning the whole history, perhaps the most important insight that emerges is the extent to which Christian life is not a blueprint but a challenge to discernment. Each age and each generation faces its own problems and questions, and these have never been solved before just because they are new problems and new questions. But a second insight that emerges is that the truly, fruitfully Christian answers to these new challenges are based on continuity of the tradition—a continuity of hope, of experience, of fellowship, of prayer, and of constant return to the sources in order to illuminate both the nature of the new questions and their relationship to the ancient faith. A third insight would seem to be the inextricably interwoven character of the personal and the societal dimensions of all the challenges that are presented to Christian spirituality: To relate well to God is to relate well among people on all levels of social complexity. To turn to God is in the last analysis to turn toward and not away from people. To acknowledge dependence upon God is to accept the full responsibility of interdependence with other people without exception and in all their needs.

When we ask whether there is a particular "usable past" for Christian women, we must acknowledge that the lives and deeds and impact of women have not been recorded and preserved for us in the same profusion as those of men. This is, of course, true of secular histories but especially so of religious histories. There are many reasons for this. Most historical interest has centered upon public life whereas the customary division of labor until relatively modern times kept the activities of most women enclosed within the family circle. The examples that are recorded for us are therefore even more exceptional than in the case of men, for whom truly ordinary lives were not recorded either. Moreover, the focus of religious histories has commonly been upon affairs of the institutional churches precisely as institutions. The systematic exclusion of women from ordination and from positions of hierarchic authority therefore guarantees that in these histories we read little or nothing about women. This is less true, however, of histories of spirituality, which have consistently taken note of monastic communities and of their outstanding members, and of lay Christians who initiated works of piety or charity or otherwise attracted attention among their contemporaries. In this there has been no reason for sexual discrimination, so that we really do have living examples in considerable detail hampered only by the fact that the literary genres of hagiography of particular periods were not always understood and appreciated in subsequent ages.

[...] It is not surprising, therefore, that when we do have records of the work and impact of Christian women on their societies, that impact tends to be prophetic, radical in its implications for the social structures of the society in the long run, and, in terms of the social dynamics, a movement from below. Examples that come to mind immediately are the many initiatives for care of the indigent sick, which led eventually to the acceptance of the idea that each society, each nation, is responsible for universal health care for its citizens without reference to their ability to pay, with all the implications for tax and insurance structures and for government intervention which that accepted belief implies. Another example is that of the many small beginnings of schooling for the children of the poor, including the orphaned and the homeless, leading as it did eventually to almost universal literacy, public school systems, and a general belief that education is a basic right for all, with the far-reaching consequences which that has for possibilities of real democracy, of economic and geographic mobility, of trade unions and other ways of broad-based participation in the shaping of the economy and the social structures. Such initiatives for health care and education, commonly taken by women who saw them as expressions of faith called forth by the immediate circumstances in which they lived, also had long-term consequences that were like slow earthquakes in all of Western society and that through colonization and international organizations have now become a challenge to the whole world.

Perhaps one of the most interesting aspects of the recorded deeds and impact of Christian women in the past is their concern for peace. From the unsuccessful efforts of Clotilde of the Franks, through a history that includes Elizabeth of Hungary, Elizabeth of Portugal, and Catherine of Siena, down to the peace protests of Dorothy Day and the women of the Greenham Common, striving for peace and reconciliation of hostile parties has been characteristic of the lives of noted Christian women. Because of their general exclusion from power, the motivation of women's peace efforts has not come from the desire for unhampered, unqualified control from a country or situation after the manner of the famous Pax Romana of ancient times. Rather, it has arisen from compassionate horror of the pain and suffering and bereavement that war causes, often to those who have the least stake in the outcome.

The all-important question, of course, is what inspiration and implications we might draw for our own times. A most significant conclusion is certainly that as long as women are systematically excluded from ordination and from the institutionalized positions of leadership and decision-making in the Church, this has some advantages as well as the more obvious disadvantages. To be deprived of the power of domination, to have little or no access to bullying power, to be unable to compel or persuade by threat or use of institutional sanctions, is necessarily to be thrown back upon other resources. And that may well be to discover that divine power, the power of grace, is of a very different kind, effective inasmuch as it empowers and liberates human freedom—freedom for self-transcendence, freedom for true community with others, freedom for God and for God's purposes in creation and history. On the other hand, to have access to bullying power is inevitably to be sorely tempted to use it. But it is not Christ's way. Because of our Church organization, Christ's way to empowerment of human freedom to transcend is likely to be more immediately apparent to women.

Looked at positively, the characteristic possibilities for a spirituality of Christian women that can really make a Christian difference in a troubled world seem to be concerned particularly with prayer, compassion, solidarity, and creative imagination. These are qualities and components that bridge the gap between the available models in the tradition of the past and the situation of contemporary women with their far greater access to positions of power and public persuasion. The opportunities are much enhanced for us in our own times, but the strictures under which our forebears worked seem in some ways to make the issues clearer. The question for us in our own times is how to make the best use both of the wider scope offered to us and of the insight that we can derive from the past with the narrower scope that is offered to women.

The challenge that many of us have come to see as immediate and difficult is that of moving beyond submissive passivity in the affairs of society without at the same time indulging in angry rejection of the traditions of our faith or in aggressively competitive self-promotion that moves against rather than with the redemption of the world. It is clearly necessary to find ways of innovating, using initiative, and exerting leadership that are not based upon personal anger and hostility and that do not seek to dominate or to seize exclusive privileges. In other words, it is necessary to avoid entering into competition for what have been seen as male prerogatives in a sinful history based upon bullying, and therefore it is necessary to discern new possibilities for quite different ways of social organization and community structures and cooperation. This calls for more than determination and aggressive energy; it also calls for contemplative sensitivity out of which new configurations can be imagined. It calls for a deeply rooted creativity.

From the beginning, Christians have known that they were called upon to do the impossible. But when we look at scripture and at the history of the Christian community, we can see a pattern in the way former impossibilities became subsequent realizations. The dynamics of the prophetic are in the creative imagination. The scriptures themselves provide rich imagery and symbolism. They are replete with stories of classic universality and with personalities that lend themselves as prototypes even across cultures and centuries. Catholic tradition has particularly appreciated and treasured this in its promotion of the sacramental principle. That is to say, Catholic tradition has taken note of the extent to which the human imagination needs to be educated in a world distorted by the consequences of sin and sinfulness.

When we look at the world about us, we never simply record what is there. We interpret. The society in which we live teaches us certain lines of interpretation according to which we consider things good or bad, normal or abnormal, more or less desirable, even more or less reasonable. The traditions, values, and expectations of our own society tend to hold us captive. In a pluralist society we may think we have escaped this because many alternatives present themselves. Yet even pluralistic society limits the range of those alternatives in ways that those within that society do not easily recognize. In a world and a history distorted by sin, the range of alternatives that a society allows is always to some extent athwart the divine purpose, but it is very difficult to imagine anything beyond or outside the permitted range. A fundamental task of Christian spirituality is imagination. It is the task of breaking the process of interpretation wide open to glimpse entirely new and different possibilities of human life and relationships.

Imagination is exercised in influential ways through literature, through the visual and performing arts, through music, but also through human relationships, social structures, technology, and science. Christian spirituality is related to all of these in two ways: it should inform them, and it should be informed by them. It should inform them not in the sense that works of art and science should be deliberately used to moralize, catechize, or set out to defend the faith, but rather that Christians steeped in the scriptures and deeply influenced by prayer and by the imperatives of charity should pursue the arts as a vocation, should engage in political process and policy, and should devote themselves to technological invention and scientific research. They need only be fully what they are and take the field seriously for what it is, and the redemption of the society through the expanding imagination will happen because the channels for redemptive grace run through us if we allow them to be open. But it is also true that the various expressions of human ingenuity in these various fields need to inform Christian spirituality and to ensure that it is dealing with the real world and the real problems of real people—to ensure that Christian spirituality is authentic and not an escape into a dream world.

WISDOM NOT RECEIVED, WISDOM NEGLECTED

Mary Collins, OSB (1987)

The gift of female human being may be to be more attuned to the word within creation because the creating God has made the female, like the ocean tides, responsive to the pull of the moon and given her ease with nature's dark places. Western religious institutions, from the days of Moses to our own, have not yet been able to receive women's spiritual wisdom and to celebrate it. We can only speculate on the reason for the Church's refusal of this gift.

The Church as we know it is an historical reality, a religious institution whose membership is male and female but whose gatekeepers, shapers, and guardians of the tradition are all males. Yet it is not inevitable that men's shaping of the tradition must draw almost exclusively on androcentric images. As Adrienne Rich has noted, "The one unifying, incontrovertible experience shared by all women and all men is that monthslong period we spent unfolding inside a woman's body. All human life on the planet is born of woman."[1]

Why, then, does the Church of Jesus Christ ignore or negate as inauthentic God imagery this universal experience of being enveloped in maternal mystery? Meinrad Craighead has painted her experiences of this feminine God as her origin and destiny, on the journey from the womb to the tomb in the recesses of the earth. What is the terror here that leads to ecclesiastical rejection of this universal experience as revelatory of divine saving presence? What fear transforms this experience into a diminished, controllable image of an enigmatically human Mary who is the Mother of Jesus and yet somehow the Mother of the race?

Only males can enter within themselves and try to name whatever terror is latent in such a revelation. But Rich suggests one possible explanation that males are "haunted by the force of the idea of *dependence on a woman for life itself*."[2] In any case, we must dare to ask what insight the Church is refusing when it refuses the female as a source of orthodox symbols of divine presence.[3]

Wisdom not received, wisdom neglected, becomes wisdom of dubious worth, finally no wisdom at all. Too many women long ago stopped believing in the worth of the gift they have. They stopped listening for the inner word of divine mystery trying to find its voice through them. Now, within these past two decades many women have begun growing in their capacity to hear the word and to recognize the embrace of divine love in their lives. But too many women are still voiceless about spiritual matters. No longer deaf to the word spoken in inner stillness, such women remain mute, unable to talk about what they have heard.

In any given culture or epoch, only a few people, men or women, have the skills to craft words and to shape images in ways that the rest of us can recognize as the truth of our own inner experience. That pair of qualities, openness to inner experience combined with uncommon skills for writing or painting, was decisive for my choice of Annie Dillard, Anne Sexton, and Meinrad Craighead as exemplars of contemporary women at prayer.

Mystics who are also poets and artists are the therapists of the imagination the Church needs today. Their creativity gives us a language for communication. Receiving their gifts, we have the opportunity for recognition: "Aha! I've been there, too," or "Oh, yes, I see.

I know," or "No, I've not met flame and ice in my own journey into God, but I trust I will not be annihilated when I do."

On the other hand, many churchgoers may be blinded by these unfamiliar visions of the living God or deaf to this new ecstatic speech. These seeming impediments are an indirect invitation to let go for a while of the God we are clinging to, whether for comfort or in anger. Unless the churches have some predisposition to inner silence and detachment from all the familiar images of God, some of us will get stuck permanently while others become increasingly alienated. The gap will grow between our life experience and our God language. We will mistrust what life itself teaches, or we will become godless because the god of the Church of Jesus Christ does not speak to our human hearts.

Feminist mystics have the courage to abandon the security and safety of what we all already claim to know about God and to respond as solitary voyagers to the divine summons to come nearer. Feminist liturgists, more daring than ecclesiastical liturgists, gather together at "the edge of the central opening" to move into unknown darkness secured and anchored to one another, rappelers ready to break each other's falls and to celebrate each other's recoveries. The churches should be cheering them on, waiting expectantly for their reports.

AWAKENING TO SILENCE

Maria Harris (1988)

When we recognize how few of our stories have been told or, when they have been preserved, how little they have been attended to, a first and fitting response is sorrow and loss, as recorded in this reflection of Rosemary Cingari:

> I have spent the past year speaking to teenagers, and using people from the Scriptures as real folks that they can grab hold of and embrace. Every time I bring up Miriam, the sister of Moses, who saved his life, without whom the

> Israelites would have had to look for another to lead them out of slavery, they have no clue as to who she is.
>
> Yes, is, not was. Miriam holds great lessons for us. What does it mean to hold life as sacred? What does it mean to use creative problem solving to deal with the impossible? What does it mean to look for what you have in common with your greatest enemy to find life and salvation? Lessons we need. Lessons as great as the ones of her brother.
>
> Miriam is part of my blood, my life, as alive for me as she was for Moses. I heard about Moses when I was five. I found Miriam when I was 30.[4]

Another response is alienation, a situation recorded by Carol Christ reflecting on the absence of women from biblical stories, where

> each woman engaged in the process of recovering her own experience will experience a deepened and deepening alienation from the traditional stories. We will no longer be content to read ourselves sidewise into stories in which 'the daughters do not exist.' We will find that self-identification with the sons and other male images and symbols in the language of the Bible and the tradition requires us to reject our particular identities as women—the very identities we are engaged in recovering and affirming in all the other important areas of our lives. [And] as our consciousness of the shapes and contours of our own experiences deepens, we will begin to realize that the exclusion of our experience from the funding of sacred stories may point to a basic defect in the perception of ultimate power and reality provided by the traditional stories.[5]

A further response, however, nourished by sorrow and loss, anger and alienation, is to realize that these insights into silences—our own and others'—have awakened us, and that the possibility of an appropriate response lies within us and within our communities. And so the coming-to, the awakening to silence throughout the curriculum can bring us to the conviction that we—teachers and students—can address the theme of silence by refusing to be silent from now on. Perhaps by ourselves at first, we can begin to practice: practice saying our own names and finding our own voices. Beginning with not-too-threatening situations and then, nurtured by courage and community in more difficult ones, we can begin to speak up "carefully listening and responding in a conversation of free selves." And in doing so we can learn something about ourselves and about our own possibilities, capabilities, and power. A character in Canadian novelist Margaret Atwood's *Surfacing* puts this response into words that have been revelatory for many women before us:

> This above all, to refuse to be a victim. Unless I can do that, I can do nothing. I have to recant, give up the old belief that I am powerless and because of it nothing I can do will ever hurt anyone. A lie which was always more disastrous than the truth would have been. The word games, the winning and losing games are finished; at the moment there are no others, but they will have to be invented; withdrawing is no longer possible and the alternative is death.[6]

Still another response, incumbent on teachers especially but to be conveyed to students as a way of empowering one another, is to learn to tune in to the silences, to wait for them, and then to address them, in ways already suggested by Adrienne Rich. "As women teachers," she tells us, "we can either deny the importance of this context in which women students think, write, read, study, project their own futures; or try to work with it. We can either teach passively, accepting these conditions, or actively, helping our students identify and resist them."[7] We can refuse to accept passivity, she tells us, in ourselves or in one another; we can give to one another the kind of cultural prodding men receive but on different terms and in different styles.[8]

But as important as any response to the generative theme of silence is the use of silence itself: not as a negative force, but as a positive one, as a healing power. For this first generative theme of Silence is multifaceted, multilayered, and richly textured. In some instances, as we have seen, silence is a demon to be exorcised. But at the same time, and from other points of view, silence—notably contemplative silence, the silence of compassionate listening—is a companion to be befriended. Silence before the mystery which holds us and cherishes us can be the power healing the wounds that other silences inflict. Powerful positive silence can lead to the discovery of the divinity within, where, like poet/playwright Ntozake Shange, we find god in ourselves and learn to love her, learn to love her fiercely.[9] Contemplative silence can be the thematic universe where we discover ourselves made in the image of this divinity and able to use her wisdom, her truth, her power as our own. If we would be wise women attending to silence that destroys, we need at the same time to be engaging the silence that creates and heals. We need to learn to recognize the presence of the One who so often comes clothed in silence, as the Still Presence, and as the Awesome Shekinah, who is ready to be our sister and our guide.

JUDAISM'S RELIGIOUS DEPTHS

Mary Boys, SNJM (1997)

One of the tragic consequences of the Christian teaching of contempt for Judaism is our blindness to its religious depth. We have only to look to splendid teachers like Rabbi Irving Greenberg to be drawn into the profundity of the Jewish holidays.[10] And, once drawn in, we may find ourselves examining our own religious practice, as I did when I read Heschel's monograph on the Sabbath. Consider the following passage:

> They who want to enter the holiness of the day must first lay down the profanity of clattering commerce, of being yoked to toil. They must go away from the screech of dissonant days, from the nervousness and fury of acquisitiveness and the betrayal in embezzling their own life. They must say farewell to manual work and learn to understand

> that the world has already been created and will survive without the help of humankind. Six days a week we wrestle with the world, wringing profit from the earth; on the Sabbath we especially care for the seed of eternity planted in the soul. The world has our hands, but our soul belongs to Someone Else. Six days a week we seek to dominate the world, on the seventh day we try to dominate the self.[11]

Heschel's reflections struck a responsive chord: I knew what it felt like to be yoked to toil (even if not manual labor), to feel as if there were no respite from work. I began to think seriously about Sabbath. Over the years I studied commentaries on the "Ten Words" (or Commandments, Exod 20:1–17 and Deut 5:6–12), read Jewish and Christian explorations of the Sabbath, noted how Jews observed (or not) the Sabbath in various ways, learned from Christians who practice Sabbath-keeping (such as many Sisters of Sion), and gave serious thought to the rhythm of work and rest in my life. I realized how readily work had become an idol in my life. I listened to the admonition of Luke Timothy Johnson: "Observe the way we organize the time and space available to us. The pattern reveals what is ultimate for us, our functional god."[12] Dorothy Bass extends Johnson's counsel:

> To act as if the world cannot get along without our work for one day in seven is a startling display of pride that denies the sufficiency of our generous Maker. To refrain from working—not every day, but one in seven—opens the temporal space within which glad and grateful relationship with God and peaceful and appreciative relationship with nature and other people can grow. Refraining from work on a regular basis should also teach us not to expect too much work from others.[13]

And so I stopped working on Sundays. I try to participate in a Eucharistic liturgy that is lifegiving rather than an obligatory "going to mass." I engage in activities that are renewing, such as meals or phone conversations with friends. I do things I find restful, like cooking, walking, reading—and yes, watching football or basketball! I try to ready my spirit for the week to come, such as attending choral vespers by candlelight at the nearby Episcopal cathedral, St. John the Divine—the equivalent for me of participating in the *havdalah* service that concludes *Shabbat* for Jews.

Jewish prayer also evokes deep resonance in me.[14] Although I do not share the intense desire to pray with Jews and to share in the life of the synagogue that a few of my Christian friends do, I nevertheless feel my prayer is enriched by what I know of Jewish prayer. For example, in one community where I lived, we took turns preparing morning prayer. When it was my turn, I occasionally used excerpts from a weekday prayer book of the Reform Jews. Our community, nearly all of whom were involved in academic life, loved to pray this together:

> A spark of the divine flame glows within us all. We give thanks for the gift of reason that enables us to search after knowledge. May our use of this gift make Your light burn ever more brightly within us.
>
> *Blessed is the Eternal Source of wisdom and knowledge.*
>
> May our pride of intellect never be an idol turning us away from You. And as we grow in knowledge, may we remain aware of our own limitations.
>
> *Blessed is the God of forgiveness and understanding.*
>
> May the beauty and mystery of the world move us to reverence and humility. O let the tree of knowledge bear good fruit for us and our children.
>
> *Blessed is our God from whom all blessings flow.*
>
> And let the consciousness of Your Presence be the glory of our lives, making joyous our days and years, and leading us to a clearer understanding of Your will.
>
> *Blessed is our God who hearkens to prayer.*[15]

Similarly, I often use Marge Piercy's poem "Nishmat"—evoking the prayer *Nishmat kol hai* ("the breath of every living thing") from the Sabbath service—for my own morning prayer. The fourth stanza alone evokes much reflection:

> We are given the wind within us, the breath
> to shape into words that steal time, that touch
> like hands and pierce like bullets, that waken
> truth and deceit, sorrow and pity and joy,
> that waste precious air in complaints, in lies,
> in floating traps for power on the dirty air.
> Yet holy breath still stretches our lungs to sing.[16]

When I study scriptural texts, I draw upon the resources of Jewish scholars nearly as often as Christian ones, and my library includes an increasing number of meditative works by Jewish thinkers such as Carol Ochs, Daniel Gordis, and David Wolpe.[17]

I have a certain reserve when it comes to using Jewish prayers and even imagery distinctive to Jewish life. Belonging as I do to a tradition that proclaimed itself the fulfillment of Judaism, I am aware that Jews may see my use of their prayers as another example of Christian appropriation of their tradition. I have participated in various rituals and liturgies in which people appropriated rituals from another's tradition—most recently from Native Americans—without regard for the context of that ritual, and I find myself increasingly uncomfortable. However well intentioned, I believe using another's rituals without a deep knowledge of their context and appropriate use manifests a lack of sensitivity. Those attracted to aspects of another's tradition need always to leaven their attraction with the virtues of spiritual regret and holy envy. Moreover, because I am not learned in Jewish liturgy, I am cautious in employing Jewish prayers beyond the privacy of my home, lest I do injustice to the context in which they are prayed. This, I believe, is a caution born of spiritual regret.

My attraction to Jewish prayer suggests that I have found Judaism a catalyst for a deeper relationship with God. In my experience, Jews are generally more reticent about God talk than are we Christians. It seems to me that at least some of this reserve follows from more explicit acknowledgment of God's presence in hiddenness. Christians, too, carry this awareness, but we tend to emphasize God's revelation in Jesus to such a degree that we are less attentive to the elusive character of the Divine Presence. I have found, for example, Everett Fox's translation of the enigmatic phrase of Exodus 3:14 (the Hebrew transliteration *ehyeh asher ehyeh* is typically rendered, "I am who am") as "I will be-there-howsoever I will be-there." Fox notes that he is following Martin Buber and Franz Rosenzweig on this; it might mean something like "my name is not a magical handle through which I can be conjured up; I am ever present."[18] His translation emphasizes the mystery of God, the One who is incomprehensible yet present in ways beyond our imagining.

God's presence as "I will be-there-howsoever I will be-there" has other dimensions that I find Judaism quite bold in addressing. A brief story speaks to my point. Last summer I spent a few days with two longtime friends enjoying theater at the Shakespeare Festival in Stratford, Ontario. During our long drives to and from Stratford, we shared aspects of our lives that our busy calendars and geographic distance from one another seldom permit us to speak about. On this particular evening, Kathleen, a historian and college president who has had cancer, asked the two of us how theologians today were thinking about Divine Providence. There was an uncharacteristic silence for quite some time. Finally, I found myself voicing the view that I had learned a great deal from Jews who refused to turn aside from the *Shoah*, who questioned God's absence from the camps, who had stared deeply into the abyss and could simultaneously interrogate God and affirm belief. I realized I had few answers to give Kathleen—only a testimony that faith in God does not preclude questioning, that belief in Divine Providence takes one into the realm of that holy insecurity of which Martin Buber spoke.[19] In retrospect, I realize how grateful I am to have encountered Jewish writers who refuse to turn aside from the difficult dimensions of faith.[20] I realize as well how appreciative I am of the Jewish tradition of arguing with God—a tradition I believe we Christians must also claim if our religious commitments are to be healthy.[21]

LITURGY, LAUNDRY, AND "WOMEN'S WORK"

Kathleen Norris (1998)

Laundry, liturgy, and women's work all serve to ground us in the world, and they need not grind us down. Our daily tasks, whether we perceive them as drudgery or essential, life-supporting work, do not define who we are as women or as human beings. But they have a considerable spiritual import, and their significance for Christian theology, the way they come together in the fabric of faith, is not often appreciated. But it is daily tasks, daily acts of love and worship that serve to remind us that the religion is not strictly an intellectual pursuit, and these days it is easy to lose sight of that as, like our society itself, churches are becoming more politicized and polarized. Christian faith is a way of life, not an impregnable fortress made up of ideas, not a philosophy, not a grocery list of beliefs.

The Christian creeds used to seem like a "grocery list" to me, and I found them very difficult to incorporate into my fledgling faith as I made my way back to church after twenty years away. But now I see them as an admirably compact form of storytelling, and this makes me glad, for story places the creeds in the realm of the daily. It is in ordinary life that our stories unfold, tales of conceiving, bearing, and giving birth, of trial and death and rising to new life out of the ashes of the old. Stories of annunciation, incarnation, resurrection, and the spirit, the giver of life, who has spoken through the prophets and enlivens our faith. As wondrous as these mysteries are, Christianity is inescapably down-to-earth and incarnational. I say "inescapably," as most of us, at one time or another, try to avoid the implications of an incarnational faith. The Christian religion asks us to place our trust not in ideas, and certainly not in ideologies, but in a God who was vulnerable enough to become human and die and who desires to be present to us in our everyday circumstances. And because we are human, it is in the realm of the daily and the mundane that we must find our way to God.

Teresa of Avila implies in her *Autobiography* that it is through other people that God chooses to reach out to us. "If Christ Jesus dwells in us...," she writes, "then we can endure all things, for Christ helps and strengthens us and never abandons us. He is a true friend. And I clearly see that if we expect to please him and receive an abundance of his graces, God desires that these graces must come to us from the hands of Christ, through his most sacred humanity, in which God takes delight." In our life of faith, then, as well as in our most intimate relationships with other people, our task is to transform the high romance of conversion, the fervor of a religious call, into daily commitment. Into the sort of friendship that transcends infatuation and can endure all things. Our desire is to love God and each other, in stable relationships that, like any good marriage, remain open to surprises and receptive to grace.

Human beings need routine. Even the homeless, I have been told by those who minister to them, establish routine as best they can, walking the same streets, foraging in the same dumpsters, sleeping in the same spots, in an attempt to maintain basic relationships with people and places. In this sense routine can be a lifesaver. But especially for those of us who have more material wealth, it can also be a depressant, a killer. People grow bored with their marriages and their jobs, their coworkers and their spouses. I have long suspected that much of the self-destructive behavior and even the suicides of people who seem to have all that anyone could want are the result of sheer exhaustion, the inability to continue in the daily round of getting more. Airplane travel can be instructive in this regard: if you want to know what is really going on in the American corporate world, spend some time listening to a young businesswoman in the seat next to you tell what it is like to feel pressured to work ninety hours a week as she also tries to be a good wife and mother. Or hear the anguish of a man in his early fifties, deemed obsolete by the company where he has worked for nearly thirty years. He has spent an entire year resisting attempts to make him quit his job before his pension would kick in. His daily routine has become a torment; there is no longer anyone among his colleagues at work that he feels he can trust. He says that his marriage and two children have been his salvation, and while he still worries about providing for his family, he has found that their unconditional love, even the children's desire to play with him when he comes home from work, is enough to get him through the day. This has sanctified his marriage and his life at a time when in most of his waking hours he has been made to feel worthless.

Ironically, it seems that it is by the means of seemingly perfunctory daily rituals and routines that we enhance the personal relationships that nourish and sustain us. I read recently in Martin Marty's newsletter, "Context," of a study that monitored the habits of married couples in order to determine what made for good marriages. The researchers found that only one activity seemed to make a consistent difference in terms of the ability to maintain a stable, happy, long-lasting relationship, and that was simple affection, the embracing or kissing of one's spouse at the beginning and the end of each workday.

Most significantly, as Paul Bosch, the author of the article, reports, "it didn't seem to matter whether or not in that moment the partners were fully 'engaged' or even sincere! Just a perfunctory peck on the cheek seemed to be enough—enough to make a difference in the quality of the relationship!" Bosch comments, wisely, that this "should not surprise churchgoers. Whatever you do repeatedly," he writes, "has the power to shape you, has the power to make you over into a different person even if you're not totally 'engaged' in every minute!"

I wonder if we might substitute that "peck on the cheek" for some of the prayers that a religious community recites daily: the Doxology, the Lord's Prayer, the Benedictus at lauds, and the Magnificat at vespers. No human being can pay full attention to the words that he or she is praying every single day, and apparently this is how God would have it. Sometimes, particularly at crisis points in our lives, we feel these words with our whole heart. They seem to burn in our chests and bring tears to our eyes. We find that we mean them in ways that remain unfathomable, and on rare occasions a new interpretation of a line or image will come to us. I will never forget the day I realized that the "you, child" of the Benedictus could refer not only to John the Baptist but to myself and to any of us who know that we are asked "to go before the Lord to prepare the way." That morning, and every morning that I pray this poem, I receive a challenge whether I consciously acknowledge it or not and an image of holiness to strive for. I am asked to share with others "the tender compassion of God" as it breaks like the dawn upon us. I am asked to cast its light "on those who dwell in the shadow of death" and allow my feet to be guided, this day and all days, "into the way of peace" (Luke 1:76, 78, 79, ELLC).

Similarly, the Magnificat summons me to hope at the end of each day, a hope that there is an alternative to the world I have been working in. A world in which I can address God, saying, "You have shown strength with your arm, / and scattered the proud in their schemes" (Luke 1:51, ELLC), a world in which the rich will come to know their emptiness and the hungry will be filled. But all too often, I pray these two magnificent prayers with only half a mind, one half yawning, only dimly conscious that it is praying, and the other half dwelling on the fact that my feet hurt and I might consider buying new shoes—perhaps even imagining their color and style—or worse, I mentally linger over some petty slight, working up an anger that distracts me from prayer. As for the words that I am dutifully saying, I might as well be praying in tongues, and maybe I am. And maybe the prayer is working despite myself.

It is a paradox of human life that in worship, as in human love, it is in the routine and the everyday that we find the possibilities for the greatest transformation. Both worship and housework often seem perfunctory. And both, by the grace of God, may be anything but. At its Latin root, perfunctory means "to get through with," and we can easily see how liturgy, laundry, and what has traditionally been conceived of as "women's work" can be done in that indifferent spirit. But the joke is on us: what we think we are only "getting through" has the power to change us, just as we have the power to transform what seems meaningless—the endless repetitions of a litany or the motions of vacuuming a floor. What we dread as mindless activity can free us, mind and heart, for the workings of the Holy Spirit, and repetitive motions are conducive to devotions such as the Jesus Prayer or the rosary. Anything is fair game for prayer, anything or anyone who pops into the mind can be included.

One prayer that I treasure, no matter what I am engaged in, comes from the great lyricist Isaac Watts in his rendition of Psalm 23, entitled, "My Shepherd Will Supply My Need." Watts interprets the ending of the psalm—"Surely goodness and kindness shall follow me all the days of my life. In the Lord's own house shall I dwell forever and ever" (Ps 22:6, GR)—not as some future event, but as existing in the light of the present, the everyday. Watts writes: "The sure provisions of my God/ Attend me all my days. O may thy house be my abode/ And all my work be praise!"

Chapter 2
The Church

LOVE AND DO WHAT YOU WILL

Denise Lardner Carmody (1999)

My own view is that necessary things are few yet utterly important. I cannot conceive of a Christian Church worthy of the name that did not subscribe to the traditional (for instance, Nicene) Creed. In the moral realm, I cannot conceive of jettisoning the Ten Commandments of Moses or the twofold commandment of Christ. In the realm of worship, I find Word and Sacrament essential to the constitution of the Church as a body of orthodox (healthy) believers. But beyond these bare bones, this necessary skeleton, most other matters admit of some flexibility. For example, the history of doctrine suggests that whether there are seven sacraments or two is less important than the conviction that Jesus left his community a tradition of breaking bread in memory of him. Similarly, it suggests that whether the community ought to have an episcopal or a presbyterian or a congregational form of government is less important than the conviction that it ought to have leaders equipped to keep it in good order. When Augustine uttered his famous line, "Love and do what you will," he was moving in the direction that I am sketching here. He did not mean that all courses of action were equally good, that no criticism was necessary. He meant that the key to right Christian behavior is love like that shown by Christ. He was reminding his hearers that without love we are likely to get lost in accidentals.

We are bound to the few essentials, the skeletal necessities like the Creed, for without them we cannot be the community of Christ. Without them we do not know who we are or what we ought to be doing. And we are bound to try to make these essential elements of our faith shape how we think about other matters, such as how we behave and how we pray. But if we commit ourselves to the Creed, to worship through Word and Sacrament, and to behavior (political, economic, sexual) that is loving, we can work out the rest well enough to be the community that Jesus intended. Our disarray will be more the untidiness inevitable for diverse, changing people than the untidiness caused by culpable ignorance, willful sin. I believe that thought experiments, forays into ideal thinking, can help us to see this distinction clearly. There is disarray and disarray, one kind right and the other kind wrong. Happy are we when we know the difference.

But, you may say, Christians have also debated about the Creed, about proper worship, and about love. True, so they have. However, I think that an ecumenical, catholic consensus has emerged historically to offer enough light to guide our way in all three areas. Since the councils of Nicaea (325) and Chalcedon (451), the main lines of the key Christian doctrines have been clear. The confession in the mainstream has been that God is a community of three unlimited "persons" who share one divine nature and that Jesus the Christ is one divine "person" with two full natures (human and divine). This confession gave voice to what a majority of the fourth- and fifth-century conciliar bishops thought had been latent in Christian discipleship from the beginning and offered the best interpretation of the Christian Scriptures (by that time the New Testament was virtually intact). Certainly, the positions of Christians with reservations about some of these formulations, such as the Arians, require serious consideration, but in retrospect their deviation from what the orthodox now consider the mainstream was relatively slight.

One can make a parallel analysis about the differences between Eastern and Western Christians in the eleventh century and between Protestants and Catholics in the sixteenth century.

They held much more in common (doctrinally, liturgically, and ethically) than they held apart. Their tragedy was that they could not love the common more than the particular, the good of the whole more than the good of their part. Today, in the broader perspective offered by the full span of the world religions, one can only weep at their narrowness. Like the Jerusalem over which Jesus wept, they did not know the things for their peace. The sobering reality, however, is that we, their latter-day descendants, have maintained much of their ignorance. We could be a much healthier body of Christ if we would accept a commonsensical view of the few essentials, grant one another wide liberty concerning the many doubtful things, and in all things make love our badge of honor.

TO SPEAK THE TRUTH IN LOVE

M. Catherine Hilkert, OP (2001)

Six centuries after her death, Catherine [of Siena's] gifts for wisdom and exhortation and her public exercise of those gifts for the sake of the Church have been publicly announced and celebrated. But the gifts of her sisters in the twentieth and twenty-first centuries have not been equally welcome. The unlettered Catherine was acclaimed as Doctor of the Church for her mystical wisdom, yet no woman has yet been named as a member of the International Theological Commission. Rarely are women asked to serve as theological advisors to bishops or bishops' conferences except, at times, on issues that are considered "women's issues," in spite of the fact that women on every continent now hold doctoral degrees in theology, including pontifical degrees. Catherine was summoned to Genoa and to Rome to counsel popes, yet canon law and documents for priestly formation in our day rule out the possibility of a woman serving as a spiritual director for seminarians. Catherine's preaching and teaching of the word inspired paupers, popes, and politicians. We are in the midst of an evangelical renewal in our own day when numerous qualified laywomen and laymen express a desire to share more fully in the Church's preaching ministry, and some bishops work to foster qualified lay preaching. Yet Vatican documents in recent years maintain that it is the priest who is properly "teacher of the Word" and that "proclaiming the Gospel is a ministry deriving from the sacrament of orders."[1]

Catherine is hailed for her loyalty to the Church in spite of her strong criticism of cardinals and corrupt clerics and her challenge to the pope to resign if he could not exercise his authority for the good of the whole Church. Yet in 1979, when Sister Theresa Kane, RSM, who was at that time president of the Leadership Conference of Women Religious (LCWR), included the following statement in her two-page welcome message to the pope, her loyalty to the Church was questioned by many:

> As I share this privileged moment with you, Your Holiness, I urge you to be mindful of the intense suffering and pain which is part of the life of many women in these United States. I call upon you to listen with compassion and to hear the call of women who comprise half of humankind. As women we have heard the powerful messages of our Church addressing the dignity and reverence for all persons. As women we have pondered these words. Our contemplation leads us to state that the Church in its struggle to be faithful to its call for reverence and dignity for all persons must respond by providing the possibility of women as persons being included in all ministries of our Church.[2]

Kane's welcome began with greetings of "profound respect, esteem and affection" from women religious throughout the country. She spoke of the inspiration of the pope's spirit of courage, his calls to attend to the needs of the poor and the oppressed, and his challenges to the United States to respond to the cry of the poor. She assured the pope of the prayers, support, and fidelity of women religious "as you continue to challenge us to be women of holiness for the sake of the kingdom," and she closed with a prayer for the pope, citing the words of the Magnificat. Nevertheless, in open letters, public apologies, and editorials, she was accused of "impertinence," "public disgrace," "wounding and dividing the Church," "perverting the

Church's teaching," "repudiating the Holy Spirit," and "being like the woman in the Garden who demands to have the 'forbidden fruit' so she will have her own will and 'be like God.'"[3] Both Catherine of Siena and Theresa Kane faced the rare opportunity and responsibility to speak publicly to a pope for the sake of the Church. Each spoke her understanding of the truth in love. (Kane chose that very phrase—"To Speak the Truth in Love"—as the title of her presidential address to the LCWR the following August in Philadelphia.) While their words inspired hope for many, their motives and wisdom were questioned by others. Neither could know at the time the impact her words and her courage would have on the history of the Church.

At the heart of Kane's plea was a call that went beyond the specifics of women's ministries, a call to listen with compassion to the voices of women. Like Catherine's proposal for a "council of the servants of God," this call to listen rests on Paul's confidence that all the parts of the body, diverse though they may be, need each other. Specifically, in terms of decision-making, a collegial, collaborative, and consultative mode of exercising magisterial authority flows from the conviction not only that individual charisms are given for the sake of the common good but also that the Spirit has bestowed the gift of wisdom on the body of believers as a whole. Vatican II described this gift as a *sensus fidei* (sense of faith)—an instinct for the authentic faith of the Church that is available only through a process of discernment that attempts to measure the authentic *sensus fidelium* (sense of the faithful). This does not refer to something that can be determined easily by polls or majority vote but rather to a process whereby faithful believing communities—including faithful women—articulate their experiences of where the Spirit is leading the Church. Jean-Marie Tillard describes this kind of corporate sense of faith or affinity for the truth using the same language that Aquinas used to describe the gift of wisdom—a "knowledge of God springing from a communion in friendship, from the intuition which the experience of the Spirit arouses."[4] The notion that the community of the baptized has a graced affinity for "right teaching" is part of a long-standing, but little emphasized, tradition in the Church. If the Spirit of Truth does indeed arouse and sustain a "sense of faith" in the community of believers, then that experience—including the experience of believing women—cannot be ignored. Women do not speak in one voice, nor should we, but our multiple experiences are part of the Church's living tradition and have a contribution to make to the authentic teaching of the Church. But the worldwide Church has yet to develop viable structures that would promote the exercise of this discernment of the authentic and living faith of the Church among the baptized.

NAMING THE PAIN IN THE BODY OF CHRIST

Mary Ann Hinsdale, IHM (2004)

Why stay in a Church that is so inhospitable to women, and that disregards (or, at best, distorts) the feminist perspective in theology? Although I have sometimes responded with an answer that has been apocryphally attributed to Rosemary Ruether—"One should stay in the Church because that's where the copy machines are!"—I find that this is a fruitful question for every Catholic to ask.

Many Catholic women have been asked to give an answer to this question. For Elisabeth Schüssler Fiorenza "staying in the Church" has to do with not giving up "the power of naming."[5] For Rosemary Ruether it is connected with her own journey into liberation and feminist theologies and the responsibility she feels to keep a deeper vision alive.[6] For writer and preacher Joan Chittister, OSB, it is a matter of recalling that "the clergy and the papacy are not the Church" and remaining committed to the vision "that sprang up in Jerusalem after the death of Jesus, formed by women in house assemblies, preached by laymen on street corners in Greece, witnessed in the whole Christian community of Jews who saw the gifts of the Holy Spirit—prophecy and tongues, discernment of spirits and healing, service and proclamation—in one another."[7]

Perhaps one of the most provocative and radical answers that I have come across, however, is that presented by feminist theologian Mary Jo Weaver. As Weaver described it in her 1993 book *Springs of Water in a Dry Land*, the choice to stay in or leave the Church is, for many women, akin to a choice between torture or starvation:

> As I have talked with Catholic women over the past ten years, I have heard stories of profound dislocation from women of all ages and in a variety of circumstances. Reduced to the simplest terms, many Catholic women find themselves in a double bind: living with misogyny and oppressive institutional structures is torture, but rejecting a church suffused with rich spiritual symbolism and a sacramental reality is starvation.[8]

Three years after posing this dilemma, Weaver wrote another article in which she admitted that her solution then was to "find strategies or to publicize efforts aimed to subvert or bypass the institution."[9] She deliberately had chosen the metaphor of desert for her book because that was where "it seemed possible to sustain oneself prayerfully within, outside of, nearby, or quite apart from the tradition," even if it meant living in "exile." Although she still found the Church to be failing many women, rather than treat the Church as virtually irrelevant, as she confesses to have done in *Springs of Water*, she decided upon a much more radical course: to revive the ancient metaphor of the "body of Christ" and to admit honestly that this body is gravely ill. It was Weaver's personal experience of dealing with cancer that led her to "wonder if some of what I have learned about my body, mind, and spirit might be usefully applied to the ecclesiastical body. Put bluntly: if the Church is the 'body of Christ,' what would it mean to talk about that body as if it had cancer?"

Reflecting on the various experiences and stages that cancer victims go through (inescapability, fear and anger, tears and grief, and finally, a healing that can only come about with our cooperation), she startles us with such statements as the following:

> Whether it is my body or the body of Christ, I cannot leave it without committing suicide....Many women in the church live in a body that has betrayed us and continues to do so. If, physically, we have managed to live in the illusion that we can control the body—dieting, medical makeover, hair coloring, endurance training—once

marked with this disease (cancer), we are quickly and inexorably plunged into the cold waters of reality.[10]

Comparing them to the dramatic route to bodily awareness that can be brought about by cancer, Weaver cites as examples of pain inflicted upon the body of Christ, the recent papal statements on women, the history of disparaging images of women in the Church, and a universal catechism that was deliberately translated into sexist language. She notes that in her dismay and anger at these events, "the temptation to sever oneself from insensitive leaders in order to escape unnecessary suffering is overwhelming."[11] So, too, is the temptation to avoidance. She finds that Paul's understandings of the ecclesial body and what it means to "have the mind of Christ" (1 Cor 2:16) have an interesting compatibility with recommendations of contemporary holistic healers, such as Steven Levine and Bernie Siegel. Levine, for instance, encourages one to sense the connections between healing and confronting the deepening experience of hurt: "Illness causes us to confront our most assiduous doubts about the nature of the universe and the existence of God. It tears us open. It teaches us to keep our hearts open in Hell."[12] Likewise, to have "the mind of Christ," according to Paul, means to be baptized into his body—his suffering body. Weaver then poses a question that might make many feminists of a certain age cringe: "Is it absurd, therefore, to believe that what we do in our physical bodies and what we suffer in the church also, somehow, completes or participates in the sufferings of Christ?"[13]

Far from advocating resignation or passivity, Weaver asks us to embrace the pain. If we do so, she believes, we will learn a new capacity for love. Citing Rowan Williams, she observes, "religion, like healing, is an experience of being unmade and remade, an experience where 'the heart is broken so as to make space for others, for compassion.'"[14] This is an experience of adult life, she continues. It is also the pattern of Jesus's life, a pattern that forms the body, the Church. Jesus "entered a world of disharmony and discord, and was able to see a larger, more inclusive pattern within it. Jesus welcomed questions and new possibilities: his community was made up of the troubled and the troublemakers whose lives and ideas befuddled the religious authorities of the day."[15]

Jesus's relationship with God "was radically new and disconcerting." As he entered more intimately into this relationship, "at the center of his heart, he found one willing to offer the divine heart as a means to transform cosmic suffering." This is what Jesus entered into, and it is what we to are called to do also. Weaver believes that healing begins first of all "with merciful awareness of the pain caused by those who live in denial of the radical openness of Jesus, who use their power to squelch the new ideas that are the spirit and mind of Christ."[16]

It is clear that in asking women to embrace the pain that the Church brings, Weaver is not advocating becoming a victim soul or indulging some sort of zealous masochism. Rather, embracing the pain means, first of all, naming the pain in this body, which "is not even permitted to think about women's ordination," which "stiffens and scowls at the notion that Christ would welcome homosexuals, divorced and remarried couples," which "requires the anguished self-denial of sexual expression for its ministers," and which "treats women from a vantage of hierarchy, privilege, emotional distance, and xenophobia." She also observes that learning to live with the cancer—whether in one's own body, or in the body of Christ—can mean that healing leads to death as well as to life. Yet, for Christians, death is not a failure. "Whether such healing practices change the institutional church or not, they touch it."[17] And in this way, connections can be made between our own bodies and the body of Christ.

As I think you can see, this is very radical! But wasn't Jesus also?

OPENING UP THE LITURGICAL MYSTERIES

Kathleen Hughes, RSCJ (2012)

What if communities across the country invited the elders among them to talk about their experience of Vatican II, about what the Church was like on the eve of the council, about the invitation of Pope John XXIII to throw open the windows, the expectations that built, the news coming out of Rome during those heady days, the documents developed by bishops from across the world with the help of their experts, addressing so many contemporary issues of urgent concern in the mid-twentieth century?

Against that backdrop, what if we talked honestly about the successes and the failures, the delights and the excesses of the sixties and seventies in the process of adopting new patterns of worship? What if we decided to start again to form ourselves in the liturgy and, at the same time, allowed the liturgy to form us in ever new ways?

I believe we need a new effort, not of liturgical catechesis but of liturgical mystagogy—a word used to describe the opening up of the mysteries for believers through reflection on actual experience. The early church made an important distinction between these two forms of teaching. When someone approached the community and asked to be welcomed into its midst, there was a prolonged period of catechesis, a time of no fixed duration when the candidate became familiar with the Christian way of life, with its teaching, its patterns of prayer, and its apostolic commitment. Candidates lived among Christians and prepared for their own profession of faith and the witness of their lives which they would promise as they joined the community.

Mystagogy, on the other hand, was less about teaching beliefs and practices. It generally took place after the experience of the sacraments of initiation and was more about helping the newly initiated go deeper into the mysteries that had been celebrated at the Easter Vigil. Mystagogy might include exploring such elements as the meaning of the darkness, the readings through the night, the experience of nakedness, the immersion into the waters of the baptismal pool, the trinitarian formula of blessing, the scent of the oil and the experience of anointing, the putting on of a new garment, the welcomed entry into a community waiting in prayer for their new members to appear, and the joy of participating fully at the eucharistic banquet.

We can learn much from this distinction between catechesis and mystagogy. In the words of the RCIA [Rite of Christian Initiation of Adults], mystagogy is understood today as the opportunity for neophytes to probe the mysteries of sacramental life:

> The neophytes are, as the term "mystagogy" suggests, introduced into a fuller and more effective understanding of mysteries through the Gospel message they have learned and above all through their experience of the sacraments they have received. For they have truly been renewed in mind, tasted more deeply the sweetness of God's word, received the fellowship of the Holy Spirit, and grown to know the goodness of the Lord. Out of this experience, which belongs to Christians and increases as it is lived, they derived a new perception of the faith, of the Church, and of the world....The distinctive spirit and power of the period of post-baptismal catechesis or mystagogy derive from the new, personal experience of the sacraments and of the community.[18]

What if we declared that all of us are still neophytes, baptized, yes, but still in need of liturgical formation, and specifically of that post-baptismal opening up of the mysteries we celebrate? What if we discerned the need for a specific period of mystagogy in our communities? What if we found ways of revisiting our sacramental experience, engaging in a holy remembering of the event, the words, the gestures, the objects, the sights and scents, the music and the silence? What if mystagogy became our bridge between experience and celebration?

This would be a new kind of liturgical formation, made up more of poetry than of prose, and it could be for the remaking of our sacramental experience if we let it work its way into our minds and hearts. What would it look like? A series of meditations, homiletic reflections, holy conversations, and poetry are among the several patterns of mystagogy available to us today.

The meditations of Romano Guardini might suggest one possibility of liturgical formation useful for today. Guardini was an intellectual giant of the liturgical movement who discovered, as a young man, the centrality of the liturgy in his own life, and who fostered it in the communities he served.

Guardini believed that liturgical formation could not be successful if it simply used a historical approach, however interesting. People did not enter into the mysteries by learning how rites came into being and under what influences. Further, he noted that liturgy was not a series of ideas requiring learned interpretation. One did not learn to love the liturgy, he believed, by being told about it. No, one learned to love the liturgy by doing it well and, in the process, learning to pay attention to the simplest of signs.

One of Guardini's books, *Sacred Signs*, contains a series of mystagogical reflections on words and gestures and objects of the liturgy that have become familiar to us, and he makes them come alive again. Here is an example, a simple reflection on making the sign of the cross:

> When we cross ourselves, let it be with a real sign of the cross. Instead of a small cramped gesture that gives no notion of its meaning, let us make a large unhurried sign, from forehead to breast, from shoulder to shoulder, consciously feeling how it includes the whole of us, our thoughts, our attitudes, our body and soul, every part of us at once, how it consecrates and sanctifies us.
>
> It does so because it is the sign of the universe and the sign of our redemption. On the cross Christ redeemed humankind. By the cross he sanctifies us to the last shred and fiber of our being. We make the sign of the cross before we pray to collect and compose ourselves and to fix our minds and hearts and wills upon God. We make it when we finish praying in order that we may hold fast the gift we have received from God. In temptations we sign ourselves to be strengthened; in dangers, to be protected. The cross is signed upon us in blessings in order that the fullness of God's life may flow into the soul and fructify and sanctify us wholly.
>
> Think of these things when you make the sign of the cross. It is the holiest of all signs. Make a large cross, taking

> time, thinking what you do. Let it take in your whole being—body, soul, mind, will, thoughts, feelings, your doing and not doing—and by signing it with the cross strengthen and consecrate the whole in the strength of Christ, in the name of the triune God.[19]

Guardini's *Sacred Signs* includes reflections on everything from doors and steps and linen to kneeling, standing, bread and wine, candles, incense, time and space sanctified, and even the name of God. The book was originally published in 1921, but prior to its publication Guardini had used these mystagogical reflections as the community gathered, before the Eucharist began. They were modest, focused meditations that he offered his assembly to deepen their knowledge and love of the liturgy and as a proximate way to prepare together for the Eucharist that was to follow.

Guardini also urged others, parents and teachers chief among them, to do their own reflections and to lead those in their care to the inner meaning of the rites. As he stated in his introduction, "whatever in human nature responds to these elementary signs should be fanned into life."[20] Guardini was intent on helping people make the connections. Indeed, he "fanned them" into flame.[21]

THE WOMEN OF VATICAN II

Catherine Clifford (2013)

Remarkably, although they were invited as something of an afterthought and were never granted the right to address the council *in aula* as were several of their male counterparts, twenty-three women took part in the [Second Vatican] council as official auditors. It was the first time in history—perhaps since the convocation of the Second Council of Nicaea in 787 by the Empress Irene, acting as regent for her son, the Emperor Constantine IV—that a woman took part in an ecumenical council.[22] Women were invited to attend the third and fourth sessions of Vatican II as auditors after a number of bishops lamented their absence.[23]

A number of laymen had been present from the middle of the first session of the council as auditors. Six of them would address the bishops on different occasions, speaking to the debates on ecumenism, on the apostolate of the laity, and on the "Pastoral Constitution on the Church in the Modern World." Notably, whenever one of these lay auditors addressed the council, the texts of their interventions were prepared and agreed upon together with all the auditors, including the women. Although none of the lay auditors had an effective vote in the council, many contributed significant elements to the drafting of the conciliar documents. Some sat on conciliar subcommissions.[24] When this was not possible, they conveyed their concerns, including critiques of the draft schemata and constructive proposals for their revision, in exchanges with receptive bishops in the wings of official debate, in both public and private meetings.

Women auditors were selected for their leadership in a number of significant international organizations for religious and laywomen. Not unlike the case of the bishops, their backgrounds and perspectives on the council and its deliberations varied widely. Marie-Louise Monnet was the first laywoman to cross the threshold of St. Peter's Basilica to attend a general congregation. She had founded a number of Catholic Action groups for youth in France and was President of MIAMSI, the Mouvement International d'Apostolat des Milieux Sociaux Indépendants. Pilar Bellosillo of Spain was the leader of the World Union of Catholic Women's Organizations (WUCWO). Rosemary Goldie of Australia was Executive Secretary of the Permanent Council for the International Congress on the Lay Apostolate (COPECIAL). Following the council, she was appointed to the staff of the Pontifical Council for the Laity, the first woman to hold a permanent post within the Roman curia. Luz Maria Longoria and her husband, José Alvarez Icaza Manero, copresidents of the Christian Family Movement, had the auspicious task of representing tens of thousands of Catholic families from around the world. To prepare for the council, they consulted members of the movement by means of an extensive survey and a thirty-six-country tour.[25]

Mary Luke Tobin, a Sister of Loretto, was the leader of the newly established Leadership Conference for Women Religious in the United States. She was joined by two other American women: Sister Claudia Feddish, Superior General of the Sisters of the Eastern congregation of St. Basil the Great, and Catherine McCarthy, president of the National Council of Catholic Women. Sister Jerome Chimy of Canada represented another Eastern Catholic religious order, the Servants of Mary Immaculate, and attended the final session of the council in the fall of 1965.

Luz and José Alvarez Icaza contributed directly to the bishops' deliberations on the ends of marriage. Their personal contributions and those of the wider Christian Family Movement weighed heavily in *Gaudium et Spes*'s treatment of the ends of marriage.[26] Sexual relations were no longer portrayed as a "remedy for concupiscence." Moving beyond the juridical approach to the sacrament that had dominated in Catholic teaching, the council now presented marriage as a mutual covenant between spouses whose self-giving love is expressed in conjugal intimacy. The unitive and procreative dimensions of marriage are presented as complementary (*Gaudium et Spes* 48, 50).

Louise Monnet contributed significantly to the text on the apostolate of the laity read *in aula* by the Englishman Patrick Keegan, president of the International Young Catholic Workers movement.[27] Economist Barbara Ward, another woman consultant, though not an official auditor, drafted significant portions of the intervention delivered by James Norris, an executive for Catholic Relief Services and a lay auditor, when he addressed the council on the issue of poverty. Following the council, Ward played a leading role as an advisor to the Pontifical Council for Justice and Peace. She would address the 1971 Synod of Bishops on Justice in the World. Lay auditors contributed significantly to the elaboration of the "Pastoral Constitution on the Church in the Modern World" and the "Decree on the Apostolate of the Laity." The religious women among the auditors, however, were not as warmly welcomed by the commission responsible for the drafting of the "Decree on the Adaptation and Renewal of Religious Life," *Perfectae Caritatis*, and were repeatedly rebuffed by its president, Cardinal Antoniutti. In all cases women were left without a direct voice. Yet their influence was unmistakable.

The council's teaching provided for several important advances and set the door ajar for more direct involvement of women in the teaching, ministry, and daily witness of the Church. The Pastoral Constitution on the Church in the Modern World (*Gaudium et Spes*) acknowledges the aspirations of women within the human community, affirming that today "women claim equality with men in law and in reality, where they have not yet reached it" (9). The constitution underlines the essential equality of women and men as the basis of social justice for all, insisting: "Since all men and women...created in the image of God have the same nature and the same origin, and since they have all been redeemed by Christ and enjoy the same divine calling and destiny, the basic equality which they all share needs to be increasingly recognized" (29). In the light of the equal dignity of women and men, any discrimination on the basis of sex is deemed "contrary to the purpose of God" (29). The council deplores the fact that women continue to be denied their basic human rights when they are the object of human trafficking (27), when they are "denied the choice of husband or state of life, or opportunities for education and culture equal to those of men" (29, cf. 60).

With regard to the participation of women in the life of the Church, the Decree on the Apostolate of the Laity (*Apostolicam Actuositatem*) declares: "Since women are increasingly taking an active part in the whole life of society, it is important that their participation in the various fields of the Church's apostolate should also increase" (9). It is recognized that laymen and women today are more deeply aware of their dignity as sharers in the priestly, prophetic, and kingly office of Christ, and of the coresponsibility in mission that flows from it. Therefore, "Laypeople with a truly apostolic mind, after the manner of those men and women who assisted Paul in the preaching of the gospel (see Acts 18:18, 26; Rom 16:3)," work in the service of their sisters and brothers in Christ. "They cooperate energetically in passing on the word of God, especially by catechetical instruction," as well as through the "care of souls" and the "administration of the church's goods" (10). To carry out these tasks, the council recognizes the need for adequate formation, including access to theological education (32, cf. *Ad Gentes* 17). These men and women who "preside over prayers" and "teach doctrine" ought to enjoy "a decent standard of living and social security" provided through a "just wage" (17). The Dogmatic Constitution on the Church (*Lumen Gentium*) acknowledges that although the majority of the baptized faithful will live their witness to the gospel in the ordinary activities of their daily lives—in caring for their families, in their daily employment at school, in factories, and offices—some men and women experience a call to devote themselves to a more explicitly ecclesial form of ministry in the service of the people of God "like the women and men who assisted the apostle Paul in the gospel, working hard in the Lord (Rom 16:3 ff)" (33).

The substance of these teachings is almost taken for granted today. At the time of the Second Vatican Council, they signified substantial progress in understanding the role of women in the life of the Church and society. These few lines of teaching opened the way for women to devote themselves to new forms of pastoral ministry and to the study and teaching of theology. In the fifty years that have transpired since Vatican II, women have come to play a major role in the pastoral life of the Church, so that today they represent the vast majority of lay ecclesial ministers in North America and in many other regions of the world. Women have also taken their place in the college of theologians, where they make significant contributions to the study of the scriptures and to theological reflection in the service of the Church and its mission.

At the outset of this chapter, we noted that the documents of Vatican II do not contain an extended reflection on the role of women as a distinct and uniquely identifiable group within the structure of the Church. This apparent silence does not mean that women's voices were ignored; rather, it confirms that they had been heard. The 1963 draft of the decree on the laity contained two articles that treated men (*De Viris*) and women (*De Mulieribus*) separately. The women at the council preferred to be considered under the inclusive heading of the generic "men" (*hominum*) over being exalted in flowery discourse or defined according to rigid categories. Pilar Bellosillo cautioned those well-intentioned bishops who, in their exuberance, were looking for ways to elaborate a poetic tribute to women. "That kind of language is detached from life and puts women on a pedestal instead of on the same level as man."[28] By using idealistic language, she argued, they actually betray an attitude that takes man to be the measure of humanity and undermines the equal dignity of women. Few women could identify with the poetic image that they were proposing. In a similar exchange, Rosemary Goldie pointed out to a commission member, "You can omit all those gratuitous flowery adjectives, the pedestals and incense, from your sentence. All women ask for is that they be recognized as the full human persons they are, and treated accordingly."[29]

The women at Vatican II understood themselves to be included fully each time the council referred to the members of the baptized faithful. During the drafting of *Gaudium et Spes,* Rosemary Goldie was invited to convey the views of the auditors on whether the council should speak concerning women. She replied in the affirmative, yet qualifying her answer: "on condition that women are not isolated as a problem apart, as it were on the fringe of society and the modern world, or as if the real problems that women experience were their exclusive concern."[30] Thanks to interventions like these by the women at Vatican II, the council's teaching refrains from adopting a theology of "complementarity" or of ascribing a set of charisms to women and another to men, one role for women and another for men. Its approach is, rather, an inclusive one. The baptized faithful are not defined according to gender roles but in accord with their participation in the mystery of Christ through baptism, a condition shared equally by all members of the Church. Any attempt to carry out a feminist reading of the teachings of Vatican II must be mindful of the council's resolve to present women as self-conscious, self-determining, and full participants in the life of the Church and society. The council's apparent silence on the question of women should not be mistaken for the exclusion of women's perspectives.

Outside the council hall at Vatican II, more militant women were beginning to raise the question of sexism and to argue in support of women's participation in ordained ministry. Their concerns were voiced by the likes of Gertrud Heinzelmann of Switzerland, who addressed a pointed petition to the Preparatory Commission entitled "Wir schweigen nicht länger" (We Will Not Keep Silent Any Longer).[31] Feminist scholars sought to build on the impulse of reform at work in the council. In the decades that followed Vatican II, many were frustrated by the speed at which debate on the question of women's ordination was preempted by Pope Paul VI[32] and Pope John Paul II.[33] While it had not created a space for a fulsome reflection on the question of women or of women in ministry, Vatican II did prepare the way for the gifts of women to be more widely recognized and welcomed into the life of the Church. However modest its advances, the council's teaching created the conditions for a significant evolution in the roles of women in the life of the Church in the postconciliar years.

Chapter 3
Holy Women

CREATOR IN THE CONVENT

Dolores Leckey (1991)

For Catholic women who did not wish to marry and have children, who sensed that their own creative impulses required a different kind of space from that of kitchen and parlor, life on the fringe of society was not a viable option. There was, however, a choice that could (and often did) support their spiritual/intellectual quest and one that conveyed a certain status: they could enter the convent.[1]

For a very long time, canon law recognized only one form of religious life for women—that of cloistered contemplative nuns with solemn vows as an authentic state of perfection. Yet dozens of new communities of women active in works of mercy and bound by simple vows appeared after the French Revolution. Their religious practice, heavily influenced by the monastic model, became a mixture of strict monastic practices and a response to contemporary need manifested in works of social compassion. These varied works themselves were a visible sign of creativity, one that will be discussed presently. But for a very long time the cloister was the premier alternative lifestyle for Catholic women and one that afforded opportunities for creative development and expression. In the twelfth century, Hildegard of Bingen, with her multifaceted giftedness, is perhaps the best-known prototype of creator-in-the-convent.[2]

Less well-known than Hildegard, but exquisitely illustrative of the connection between creativity and the convent, is Sor Juana Inés de la Cruz, widely regarded by critics of Spanish literature as one of the great poets of seventeenth-century New Spain—Mexico. For centuries she has puzzled many who studied her life and her accomplishments.

Juana Inés lived at the royal court in Mexico City from ages sixteen to twenty, a favorite of the Vicereine. Her beauty, intellectual acumen, and literary gifts were greatly admired. By all accounts she lived fully the life of the court, participating in entertainments and diversions, including flirtations and amorous theatrical plays. At the height of her courtly pleasures, at age nineteen, she entered a cloistered Carmelite convent, but after a brief time there, she returned to the world, probably because the Carmelite way of life was too rigorous for her. But a year and a half later, she took her vows in an order much milder in discipline, the Hieronymite Order.

Mexican writer and Nobelist Octavio Paz, in his stunning study of this extraordinary woman, considers the possible reasons for this unexpected and hard to explain decision in her life.[3] First there is her background. She was "illegitimate" and so did not have the security of family and dowry (although she knew her mother's family and was indebted to her grandfather for sparking her love of learning). But her irregular family situation and the consequent lack of dowry was an obstacle to a suitable marriage. Still, she was well regarded at court, and who knows what might have been arranged? Paz lays the family situation aside. He sees a different reason.

While it seems quite reasonable to him that she might have fallen in love while she lived in the palace, and while it is indisputable that she lacked family position and a dowry, her choice of the convent does not seem "second best" to Paz. Juana herself gives what to Paz is a most plausible reason for her choice: she felt no inclination toward marriage.

Paz is careful to make a distinction between love and matrimony, which, in the seventeenth century, were quite separate. There are women, he reminds us, who choose to avoid the married state, which does not, however, rule out love. But marriage at that time and in those circumstances was not conducive to the pursuit of the intellectual, artistic, aesthetically creative life. While not denying the authenticity of Sor Juana's religious vocation, he situates it in a human context, namely, the need to find a haven for herself to develop her talents, a place respectable and secure. Her eagerness for knowledge was paramount. She writes in a document called *Response* the following passage:

> And so I entered the religious order, knowing that life entailed certain conditions (I refer to superficial, and not fundamental, circumstances) most repugnant to my nature; but given the total apathy I felt toward marriage, I deemed convent life the least unsuitable and the most honorable I could elect if I were to ensure my salvation. To that end first (as, finally, the most important) was the matter of all the trivial aspects of my nature…, such as wishing to live alone, and wishing to have no obligatory occupation to inhibit the freedom of my studies, nor the sounds of a community to intrude upon the peaceful silence of my books.[4]

Paz categorizes her reasons, then, as negative (her antipathy toward marriage and her need for a refuge from the difficulties of a woman alone in the world) and positive (her attraction for learning). As a child she steeped herself in her grandfather's library, devouring books, all kinds of books, unknown to her family. That love of knowledge deepened with the years. To be faithful to the inner call to know and to write, she needed something that the convent could offer—solitude. It was not a solitude of total isolation but one that allowed for intellectual communication. Sor Juana was engaged in a far-ranging and continuing correspondence with the outside world for which, it must be admitted, she was censured. Still, the right combination of solitude, communication, and learning was available to her in the convent of St. Jeronimo.

The dynamics of solitude and a community of shared interest are, I believe, essentials to the creative life. Solitude, as the poet May Sarton notes, "cracks open the inner world."[5] Creative leaders, thinkers, artists—these seem especially marked and strengthened by solitude. Catherine of Siena in her room voluntarily cut off from the social intercourse of her home, John of the Cross in the Tower, Florence Nightingale on her sickbed, Malcolm X in solitary confinement, Van Gogh in Arles, Nelson Mandela in a South African prison, and of course, Jesus in the desert—for all these and so many more, unseen solitude offered a spaciousness where the secrets of the soul could be explored and given form. Sor Juana's convent was such a place. But there was a level of contrast present also.

In many ways St. Jeronimo resembled a small city. Each nun had a cell that was in reality a small apartment complete with kitchen, bathroom, and sitting room and often occupying two floors. Servants and slaves (who could be sold) were part of the tiny households within the larger organization of the convent. Even the habits—conventual dress—were more elegant than humble. Jewelry often was worn. Visitors (theologians, homilists, members of the court, in addition to family) were frequent, remaining in special "speak rooms" after vespers. Visits sometimes inspired performance of some type—dancing, singing, recitation, theatrical scenes, usually performed by the girls studying with the nuns. It would seem that visitors were refreshed in the style of the true salon.

Religious structure was, of course, observed. There was a daily horarium of prayer that included Mass, Lauds, the daytime hours of prayer, Vespers, and Compline. The prayer moments were, in fact, the substance of the nuns' common life. Meals were rarely taken in common, the nuns preferring their cells and the culinary skills of their particular servants. Apparently time was available for individual interests such as sewing, painting, and crafts. In Paz's view these and other avenues of continued learning and creative expression were essential for mental health in the convents. And while the convents of New Spain were not on par with the monasteries, or particularly with the Jesuit houses of study, according to Paz, for someone with Sor Juana's intellect, energy, and aesthetic sensibilities, her convent was uniquely suited to her development. Poetry and plays, secular and religious, flowed from her cell and were carried beyond the borders of Mexico. Most of her work was published in Spain and was recognized then, as now, as something of value. One sees this first in her sonnets. Paz calls attention to the sonnet images, which transcend time and cultures. One remarkably modern image is that of the writer who sees herself writing:

> Unhappy lyre whereon your music played,
> be still, its echoes call to you in pain,
> misshapen are the letters that here fall,
> black teardrops from my melancholy pen.[6]

Sor Juana matches May Sarton's delineation of the poet as one who lives a life of disciplined awareness so that everything may be met with an innocent eye, a state of being on the edge of mysticism.[7] Years of Lauds and Vespers help to expose one's being. But the prayer of the Church, the seclusion of her cell, and stimulating correspondence were not all that nourished Sor Juana's inner life and light. Like Sarton centuries later, the poet Sor Juana developed through the friendship of women, within and without the convent.[8] Not only did these friendships fulfill psychic needs but probably ushered in Sor Juana's Muse as well.

More startling than her twentieth-century poetic images, her volume of work, and her web of relationships were Sor Juana's feminist writings, almost impossible to imagine in the seventeenth century in a society whose ethos was shaped by a combination of Arabic and Roman-Christian beliefs and customs regarding women.[9] In one poetic satire Sor Juana questions the dual standards applied to women and men regarding sexual behavior. Why do men insist on blaming women, she asks? Does not the sexual act almost inevitably result from masculine initiative? She was not the first person to raise these arguments, but she was the first woman of literature to do so with intelligence and grace. "There is nothing similar in literature by women in the 17th century France, Italy, or England," says Paz.[10]

Her feminism reached beyond sexual behavior, however. She wrote admiringly of learned women, those of pagan times as well as Christian times. In defense of her own pursuits of learning under scrutiny by the Holy Office, she addressed herself to the question of what the Pauline text about women keeping silent in the churches really meant, and she concluded that women may study, interpret, and teach Holy Scripture, although not from the pulpit but rather in their homes and in private places. And, in fact, she argues for something akin to universal education for women to include secular subjects as well as sacred ones.[11] Sor Juana's life and work invite further study and reflection.

REMEMBERING GUADALUPE'S PROMISES

Jeannette Rodriguez (1996)

In many ways cultural memory can be likened to tradition in that tradition passes on a world of meaning from generation to generation. Tradition, as well as cultural memory, carries all these experiences, personal as well as communal, to the people. Implicit and explicit understandings, myths, stories affect anything that actualizes the potential of the human person. Charles Davis notes:

> A tradition is a way of responding to reality including feelings, memories, images, ideas, attitudes, interpersonal relationships; in brief, the entire complex that forms life within a particular world, a world bonded by a horizon that determines the particular sense of reality that pervades it.[12]

Tradition has two distinct parts: the process, the actual handing on of tradition, and the *traditium*, the content and product. In other words, tradition could be both a participle (remembering) and a noun (a memory). The participle and noun are two sides of the same coin. Cultural memory has the same two elements attributed to tradition. It is both remembering and a memory. Cultural memory is remembering, tradition, the process. Who remembers? A people within a culture. An individual within a group. It is the people or the individuals that carry a memory. How is it remembered? Memory, oral and written accounts, celebrations, sacred space—all contribute to cultural remembering. What *traditium* is being remembered? What does this memory do? What does it evoke? What are its manifestations?

Cultural memories are manifested in affectivity, ideas, aspirations, beliefs, stories. In my book *Our Lady of Guadalupe: Faith and Empowerment among Mexican-American Women*, I identified Our Lady of Guadalupe as a cultural memory.[13] The memory of Our Lady of Guadalupe is carried and transmitted in the stories Latina women share and by the devotions that express faith in her. Cultural memory is contained in the image of Guadalupe itself; it is recorded in the Aztec document entitled "Nican Mopohua." In the celebrations on Our Lady's feast in December, Guadalupe is made present. The remembering and evoking are mainly a matter of feelings and aspirations, of searching for hope and strength. A memory, like Guadalupe, is carried by a people in their historical, social, and political world. In a culture, a social group consciously and unconsciously passes along value-laden memories. This memory of Our Lady of Guadalupe passes on the value of self-worth, of appreciation of one's own culture and tradition. The image and message of Our Lady of Guadalupe, therefore, are vehicles for cultural memory. As cultural memory, Guadalupe evokes an affectivity that bonds individuals not only to her but to each other, thus becoming a key element in their sense of being a community of people.

Cultural memory bears similarities to both historical memory and myth. Like historical memory, cultural memory is rooted in actual events and in the surrounding and resulting alignment of images, symbols, and affectivity that are even more pervasive than "facts." Many kinds of historical memories are transmitted through text, oral history, tradition, plays, personal and collective memory. Occasionally, historical memories are so overwhelmingly important that they define the essence of a people and are imperative to their survival. An implied distinction could be highlighted here. "Historical memory" tends to be constructed to support those in power. Cultural memory can either support the dominant culture or, as with Guadalupe, subvert it by empowering the marginalized cultures.

Unlike myth, cultural memory has a historical basis; however, like myth, it can be transformative. It has power to influence human life. Wendy O'Flaherty tells us:

> A myth is a story that is sacred to and shared by a group of people who find their most important meanings in it; it is a story believed to have been composed in the past about an event in the past...an event that continues to have meaning in the present because it is remembered; it is a story that is part of a larger group of stories.[14]

The transforming characteristic attributed to myth is also characteristic of the process of cultural memory. **Cultural memory transmits an experience rooted in history that has reached a culturally definitive transformative status.** The myth/story of Guadalupe is a cultural memory because it "enshrines the major hopes and aspirations of an entire society."[15]

Cultural memory does not necessarily originate from a calamity, but most often it does arise out of events that are transformative, that bring about recognizable shifts in the world of meaning of a people. Cultural memory fulfills the need to transcend certain events or circumstances (the Jewish people and the Holocaust) and/or to maintain a corporate identity such as an historical event used to create patriotism (the American Patriots and the Boston Tea Party; Mexican identity and Guadalupe). This memory passes from generation to generation, from parent to child, from leader to follower, through oral traditions, written accounts, images, rituals, and drama. Cultural memory is evoked around image, symbol, affect, or event precisely because it keeps alive and transforms those events of the past which continue to give meaning to the present.

The Guadalupe event is rooted in history. It has a given content. Like all memories, cultural memory changes over time. Culture is a living and dynamic reality. Memory contributes to the defining and redefining of a given culture. This holding on to, passing on, and reinterpreting the memory is both an intellectual and affective process.

What theological insights can be gathered from the cultural memory of Our Lady of Guadalupe? First, from a theological perspective, memory serves as an "expression of eschatological hope" and a "category of the salvation of identity."[16] Johann Baptist Metz takes this approach in his fundamental theology, where he states that memory, especially as "the memory of suffering," is the basic concept in a theological theory of history and society.[17] Metz argues that "memory can have a very decisive ecclesiological importance in defining the Church as a public vehicle transmitting a dangerous memory in a system of social life."[18] Guadalupe represents an eschatological hope for those who believe in her. Guadalupe reminds us that the way the world is, is not the way it was meant to be. Therefore, to uphold the memory of the Guadalupe event shows "solidarity in memory with the dead and the conquered."[19] The dead and the conquered Nahuatl people, Latina women, all oppressed and marginalized people, may be resurrected in the Guadalupe event. The Guadalupe event reminds us that the manifestation of the divine takes her stand with the marginalized and oppressed and shows them love, compassion, help, and defense. The Guadalupe event, memory, story, recalls who we are as a people, how we have been oppressed, and how God sides with the poor and calls us all to liberation and healing.

The cultural memory of the Guadalupe event exists because there is a need for it to exist. Succinctly, Guadalupe as cultural memory continues to exist because it feeds a basic need for identity, salvation, hope, and resistance to annihilation. The Guadalupe story speaks of the restoration of human dignity in a voice once silenced and now restored. It speaks of the restoration of a lost language and a way of perceiving the divine. It speaks of assessing lost symbols and transforming them in a new time. Ultimately, it speaks and continues to speak of a shared experience of a people—a people that suffers.

God is faithful to the covenant promise that God is *our* God and we are God's people. Guadalupe is a manifestation of this biblical covenant. Metz states:

> Christian faith can be understood as an attitude according to which man remembers promises that have been made and hopes that are experienced as a result of those promises and commits himself to those memories.[20]

This is what a devotee of Guadalupe does. The devotee, through cultural memory, remembers the promises of compassion, help, and defense that Guadalupe initially made. These promises are experienced by the people as hope, a hope carried in and expressed through cultural memory, retelling the story, celebrating the feast, visiting the Basilica, praying before the Virgin's image, and working for justice. As a result of these promises the devotee is committed to the Guadalupan memory and image, that which can be read, touched, felt, seen, experienced. What other memories, images, insights have been transmitted consciously or unconsciously?

HENRIETTE DELILLE'S SUBVERSIVE LOVE

M. Shawn Copeland (2007)

In the morally foul atmosphere in which black female bodies were debased, surely Henriette Delille questioned the meanings of passion and desire. All around her women and men claimed to be falling in and out of love, accepted societally determined roles, and involved themselves in commercial transactions that parodied love. Surely she found this disillusioning, tasteless, and offensive. Like all human beings, she yearned to love and to be loved, yearned for genuine passionate encounter. Such longings are normal aspects of human nature and are wholesome and holy. The wisdom of centuries of Christian living teaches that these human longings are met only by the love of God, by union with the divine.

Let us suppose, then, that after an intense religious experience, Henriette Delille turned away from temptation to easy love and easy loves; she fell in love with God. Falling in love with God is "other-worldly falling in love."[21] To fall in love with God is to fall in love with Someone transcendent, Someone who draws us toward self-transcendence, Someone who has a passion for human beings.[22] Henriette Delille responded to this divine passion, this gratuitous love by the free gift of her self—mind, heart, soul, and body "without qualifications, conditions, or reservations."[23] Certainly, her response may be associated with what theologians for centuries have named the "natural desire to see God." Yet, we ought not to discount or dismiss her longing desire, her passion for something more, for Someone. Henriette Delille may never have read Augustine, but she would have resonated with his declaration of love: "O God, you have made us for yourself, and our hearts are restless until they rest in thee."

God's passionate love dismantled and abolished the horizon that heretofore had shaped her concern and interest, drew her ever more deeply into the divine self, opened, expanded, and flooded her heart. God's passionate love transformed not only what she desired but her very desiring self. Her deepest desires were fulfilled, "for being in love with God [is] the ultimate fulfillment of [our] capacity for self-transcendence."[24] Delille's experience of God's passionate love gave rise to a desire for new and transformed valuing, choosing, acting, and living. We do not know what Henriette Delille experienced, but as John of the Cross tells us, "Once the taste and savor of the spirit is experienced, everything carnal is insipid."[25] What we do know is that she was prompted to write: "I believe in God. I hope in God. I love. I [desire] to live and die for God." These are the words of a person in love with God. They signify what Carmelite Constance FitzGerald describes as "a decisive, preferential choice of the heart for God, a conscious shift in one's focus of meaning which ever so slowly redirects and claims desire."[26]

"Being-in-love is a subjectivity transformed."[27] In other words, God's love worked in Henriette Delille a transformation that gave birth to new values, new hope, new possibilities. Perhaps she "experience[d] the inner fire and the inner light…the living flame of love that [made her] being to be *being-in-love*."[28] One way of embodying response to love of God is voluntary consecrated chastity.[29]

The practice of sexual abstinence has deep roots in Judaism and Christianity—Jews for the sake of Torah study, Christians in imitation of Christ.[30] New Testament scholar Sandra Schneiders contends that first- and second-generation Christian women who claimed virginity for explicitly religious reasons were "seen as a dangerous challenge to patriarchal social structures of both family and state."

> Women who declared themselves unavailable as reproductive agents to carry on the family name, seal interfam-

> ily alliances, or provide the future citizens of the Empire because they were "married to Christ" were refusing not only their species role, but also their assigned social role as property of men and state.[31]

As a gesture of personal autonomy and control of the body, virginal commitment may be read as radical, even protofeminist. But, as Schneiders asserts, these women "were in fact giving absolute priority to their own spiritual agenda in the face of overwhelming pressure to the contrary."[32]

Henriette Delille and the free black women who gathered as the Congregation of the Sisters of the Presentation understood societal and familial pressure to conform to the social norms of their caste and class. Although, in their earliest and informal phase, the women did not declare formal religious vows as the group evolved toward a protoreligious congregation, both Davis and Gould think that the women quite likely took private vows. But even in the group's first phase, Delille prepared directives that counseled members toward "gentleness and prudence," "edifying example," and the avoidance of "serious failings" that could give rise to scandal. Should a member refuse to heed a thrice-repeated "charitable" admonishment, her name was to be removed from the membership register of the Congregation.[33]

Provision for correction would not have been uncalled-for. French-born American-trained priest Michael Portier organized a confraternity of *young gens de couleur libres* in 1817 to evangelize and instruct the enslaved people. Writing to the rector of the Grande Seminaire in Lyon, Portier boasted of the young people's fervor ("They wear a red ribbon and a cross and they promise to fight daily like valiant soldiers of Jesus Christ") and fidelity "in Babylon, in the midst of scandals."[34]

The quality and power of consecrated chastity as lived by free black women would have had a sharp countercultural impact in the context of slavery and *plaçage*. The prevailing ideology of slavocracy stigmatized both enslaved and free black women as inherently immoral; at the same time, *plaçage* was steeped in an ambiguous morality that tainted all involved. Emphasis on avoiding occasions of temptation, on modesty, even on bodily deportment and simplicity in dress would have been common to any society of pious women. In this particular social context, adverting to outward signs of restraint in personal comportment may have been imperative. But consecrated chastity as the reservation of one's person, one's body is neither privation nor concession; rather, it is a form of self-transcendence. Moreover, consecration of the heart, the serious, quiet cultivation of an interior life of prayer, might be of equal if not greater importance.

Love of God forms the ground of human authenticity, of self-transcendence; cognitive, moral, and practical liberation are rooted in this love. Christian witness with its concrete intersubjective and interpersonal dimensions is essential to this love.[35] Christian witness demands an engagement with bodies, not their denial; a struggle with history, not surrender to it. The Sisters of the Presentation sought to live this engagement and struggle in imitation of the first Christians: "Now the whole group of those who believed were of one heart and soul, and no one claimed private ownership of any possessions, but everything they owned was held in common" (Acts 4:32). The women devoted themselves to care of the infirm and poor, prayer and praise, instructing others in the faith, sharing all things in common—constituting themselves as an *ekklesia*, an assembly of the baptized.

By 1894, the "little flock" begun as the Sisters of the Presentation were known as the Sisters of the Holy Family and deeply embedded in the religious and cultural fabric of New Orleans. Thirty-two years earlier, Mère Delille had died relatively unknown, "except by the poor and the insignificant."[36] Was she the seed that had fallen into the ground so that it might give life? In that same year, Sister Mary Bernard Deggs was asked to write an account of the early period (1842–1883) of the foundation. Deggs shapes her memoir around the lives of the earliest superiors—Delille, Gaudin, Charles, Mother Marie Magdalene Alpaugh, Mother Marie Cecilia Capla, and Mother Mary Austin Jones.

Mère Delille left her sisters a legacy of paramount service to the enslaved and poor; she committed them as well to the embrace of holy poverty. Deggs recounted several anecdotes of the sisters' material privation:

> Many were the times that the foundresses had nothing to eat but cold hominy that had been left from some rich family's table. It is not necessary to say a word about their clothing, for it was more like Joseph's coat that was of many pieces and colors darned, until darn was not the word.[37]

And again:

> Many a night did our dear sisters, after working all day, pray that some dear friend would send them a few spoonfuls of sugar. One time a servant came with a silver waiter with what one might call a grand dinner. Others sent us bundles of candles. Others came with a few pounds of coffee and others, if the weather was cold, with a wheelbarrow of wood and of nut coal. Many ladies, knowing how poor we were, often sent us old shoes or boots to wear in the yard when it rained.[38]

Courage also was included in Mère Delille's legacy. Deggs remembered that after emancipation some free people of color, former slaveholders, importuned the sisters to terminate religious instruction to the newly freed people.

> That was asking too much of our sisters, for our dear Lord said, "Go and teach all nations" (Mt 18:19–20). We, as sisters, are more obliged than others to teach all to know their God. And the day that we would refuse would be the day of sin for us, for our dear Lord said in another place that He had not come for the just, but to save sinners (Mt 9:13; Mk 2:17, Lk 5:32). This would have been preaching one thing and practicing another.[39]

But the sisters equivocated, if agonizingly so, when asked by that same class of people to separate their children from the children of emancipated slaves.

Yet, an astonishing example of love's subversive power may be found in another anecdote in which Deggs described the purchase in 1870 of a building for St. Mary's School. During the period of enslavement, this building and its grounds, located on Chartres Street, had served as a trader's slave pen.

> After the late war, many in this city looked on the old house as a disgraceful place and it was abandoned. No one would think of buying it for the very reason that it had previously been a trader's yard and many sins had been committed at that place, not only sins, but the most horrible crimes. It must have been God's will that our sisters should buy this place to expiate the crimes that had been committed there.[40]

Here, enslaved black women and men were packaged and displayed, examined and handled, assessed and purchased—their value turning on a calculus of profit and pleasure. Could such a dwelling be capable of exorcism, of redemption?

Expiation calls for remorse, contrition, amendment of purpose and performance, and change of heart. We expect, perhaps even require, those who have committed offenses or done grievous wrong to work out recompense in sincere sorrow, amend behavior, and live concretely into and out of change of heart. What might it mean for Deggs to link the purchase of this property by the Sisters of the Holy Family to the idea that God wills black women to expiate the heinous sins committed against black women (and men)?

Chattel slavery, the war that contributed to its demise, its discriminatory aftermath, and *plaçage* comprise at least two centuries of maldistributed, transgenerational, negative, massive suffering for black women and men.[41] These cruel and public events brought black and white, female and male, religion and culture, economy and policy face to face with a situation that defies human imagination and calls for uncommon religious, intellectual, and moral resources. Such congealed evil in society may be understood as "societal impasse."[42] Societal impasse calls for as much remorse and repentance, healing and creativity, mercy and justice as we human beings can muster. Perhaps even more was required of the daughters of Mère Delille. "This is my commandment, that you love one another as I have loved you" (Jn 15:12).

> Love your enemies, do good to those who hate you, bless those who curse you, pray for those who abuse you....If you love those who love you, what credit is that to you? For even sinners love those who love them....Your reward will be great, and you will be children of the Most High; for he is kind to the ungrateful and the wicked. Be merciful, just as your Father is merciful. (Lk 6:27–28, 32, 35b–36)

Delille left her daughters a legacy of love—love, powerful and subversive; love that is self-transcending; love that brings good out of the injury of evil.

> Love is patient; love is kind; love is not envious or boastful or arrogant or rude. It does not insist on its own way; it is not irritable or resentful; it does not rejoice in wrongdoing, but rejoices in the truth. It bears all things, believes all things, hopes all things, endures all things. Love never ends. (1 Cor 13:4–8a)

To the pain and problem of evil, to societal impasse such love poses a transcendent solution, and that solution is patterned in the passion, death, and resurrection of Jesus of Nazareth who is the Christ of God. Such love absorbs the unintelligibility, the irrationality of the sin of enslavement—objectification, physical assault, sexual exploitation, manipulation, and psychic battering of human beings. Such love meets evil with good, breaks the cycle of violence and oppression. Meeting evil with good and with love calls for living into and out of divine grace gratuitously offered; calls for openness and cooperation with that grace in personal, psychic, intelligent, moral, intersubjective, and religious development; calls for drawing the supernatural resources of faith, hope, and charity.[43]

Thus, love and prayer as active cooperation with divine grace might hallow the ground where black women had been forced to endure the pornographic gaze of sellers and buyers of human flesh. Love and prayer as cooperation with divine grace might purify the place where black women had been handled, assaulted, and raped. Love and prayer for enslaved women (and men), love and prayer for those who sold, bought, forced, and violated them.

Was love and prayer effective, fruitful? From this dreadful site, Deggs tells us, came "one of the most successful houses that the Holy Family Sisters ever had since its foundation."[44]

MADELEVA'S CREATIVE RESPONSIBILITY

Anne E. Patrick, SNJM (2009)

Responsibility's passive dimension has been greatly stressed in Catholic literature, whereas there has been much less emphasis on creative responsibility, which involves the ability to think independently and to take risks for the sake of helping to improve life for oneself and one's neighbors. Both types of responsibility are needed, like the black and white keys on the piano. The problem is that socialization has equipped many of us too well for the one and very poorly for the other. Women and men alike have received moral training that denies or minimizes the agent's role in recognizing obligations and in balancing obligations that conflict. Many women, however, face particular challenges insofar as the socialization of females has tended to foster passivity and stifle growth toward exercising power and original thinking.[45]

And yet we do have many instances of women who have exercised creative responsibility. Dorothy Day, cofounder with Peter Maurin of the Catholic Worker Movement, comes to mind, as does Mother Alfred Moes, OSF, a key figure in the founding of the Mayo Clinic. After a tornado had devastated the frontier town of Rochester, Minnesota, in 1883, this community leader persuaded Dr. William W. Mayo to staff a hospital if she would build it. With the support of her religious community, she could deliver on this promise, and she raised enough funds to open St. Mary's Hospital in 1889. In 1894 Dr. Mayo testified to the importance of her initiative, for he had at first been reluctant to change his medical practice. Speaking of the conversation that led to the hospital, he observed:

> The Mother Superior came down to my office and in the course of the visit she asked, "Doctor, do you not think a hospital in this city would be an excellent thing?" I answered, "Mother Superior, this city is too small to support a hospital." I told her that the erection of a hospital was a difficult undertaking and required a great deal of money, and moreover we had no assurance of its success even after a great deal of time and money had been put into it. "Very well," she persisted, "but you just promise me to take charge of it and we will set that building before you at once. With our faith and hope and energy, it will succeed."[46]

There is a gospel parable that can encourage us to emulate such women as Mother Alfred Moes and to become more creatively responsible selves. This is the Parable of the Talents from Matthew's Gospel (25:14–30). This story immediately precedes the narrative of the Last Judgment (25:31–46), in which Jesus rewards the faithful with the words, "I was hungry and you gave me food, I was thirsty and you gave me drink" (v. 35a). In the Parable of the Talents, three servants are given different sums of money as their master departs for a trip. The servant who received the least amount buried his money out of fear. The other two servants risked investing their talents, and their money doubled in value. In the end these creatively responsible servants are rewarded while the timid, fearful servant does not fare so well. This fearful servant reminds me of someone who sees the moral life only as a matter of not breaking the rules. And we might interpret the difference between the two and the five talents as symbolizing the different levels of creative responsibility, what [psychologist Mihaly] Csikszentmihalyi distinguishes as everyday personal creativity, or creativity with a lowercase *c*, and eminent or culture-changing creativity, demarcated by an uppercase C.

My grandmother, Stella Farrell Flynn, was probably closer to the lowercase form of creativity when she found a way to feed her eleven children during the Depression of the 1930s and still had something for the unemployed men who came to their kitchen door hungry. Dorothy Day, on the other hand, is recognized as having made a lasting change in Catholic and urban culture, and Csikszentmihalyi would regard her as eminently creative. Like Dorothy Day and Mother Alfred Moes, Sister Madeleva is another instance of eminent creativity, and her life also helps us appreciate the way creative responsibility is related to institutional and social life, or "domains" and "fields," as Csikszentmihalyi calls them.

Madeleva's personal creativity showed itself in many ways—her poetry, her teaching, her correspondence, her essays, and her autobiographical writings, to mention a few. To my knowledge, however, she did not introduce lasting novelty into the domains of literature or pedagogy so that we can say they will never be the same as a result of her efforts. But I think we can say that her creativity with respect to the Sister Formation Movement and the School of Sacred Theology at Saint Mary's College was of the eminent or culture-changing variety.

What she catalyzed with her efforts to ensure that teaching sisters received professional training before being sent into the classroom has had an enormous and lasting impact, not only on the religious congregations involved but on American Catholic culture as a whole. In her 1997 biography of Madeleva, Gail Porter Mandell stresses the importance of a panel she had organized for the National Catholic Education Association in 1949, which included groundbreaking papers by Madeleva and several others that were later published under the title *The Education of Sister Lucy*.[47] Three years later, Mandell notes, the first national gathering of U.S. religious took place in August 1952 at the University of Notre Dame, and this "formed the link between the ideas published in *The Education of Sister Lucy* and the actual Sister Formation program, established in 1954."[48]

Likewise, the innovation of opening Saint Mary's School of Sacred Theology in 1943, which had resulted from Madeleva's interest in providing education for teachers of religion, was of the culture-changing variety. Today we tend to forget how dramatic a change it was when women first gained the credentials for teaching theology at the college and graduate levels, but it was the program started by Madeleva that first made it possible for non-clerics to earn graduate degrees in Catholic theology. According to the 1982 directory of the Catholic Theological Society of America, all the women members with PhD degrees from the 1950s had studied at Saint Mary's College. Among them was Margaret Brennan, IHM, who earned her doctorate in 1953 and, later, as leader of her congregation, systematically encouraged younger sisters, including Madeleva lecturers Sandra M. Schneiders, IHM, and Mary Ann Hinsdale, IHM, to pursue advanced studies in theology.[49] Besides her work in community administration, which included service as president of the national Leadership Conference of Women Religious in 1972, Brennan taught numerous graduate students during twenty-five years as a professor of pastoral theology at Regis College of the University of Toronto.[50] Another eminent graduate of Saint Mary's School of Sacred Theology was Mary Anthony Wagner, OSB, who completed her PhD in 1957 and taught theology at the College of St. Benedict and St. John's University in Minnesota for thirty-seven years. With Paschal Botz, OSB, she cofounded the Benedictine Institute of Sacred Theology there for non-clerics and was associate dean for ten years. In 1974 this institute merged with the seminary at St. John's to become St. John's University School of Theology, and Wagner was its first dean, serving until 1978. She later edited the national publication *Sisters Today* from 1979 until its last issue in November 2000.

[…] Both these influential efforts illustrate the social-institutional side of creativity. We might suppose that the School of Sacred Theology and the Sister Formation Movement were sudden inspirations that came from nowhere to Madeleva's convent room, perhaps as she was writing a poem or tying her shoelaces. But the process was more complex, as Mandell's biography makes clear, and it was much more *social* than the stereotype of the solitary creative genius suggests. In terms of the creative process, Madeleva had greatly desired to improve religious education and do better justice to the talents of women religious; she had done considerable preparatory work before coming up with her remarkably productive ideas; and the issues were incubating as she went about other tasks and talked with her friends. The insights may seem to have come suddenly, but they came to a well-prepared mind and to a moral agent who knew how to engage others in effecting change for the good.

With respect to the School of Sacred Theology, Mandell shows that Madeleva's creativity here depended very much on her social life and her involvement with the Holy Cross Sisters, the National Catholic Education Association (NCEA), and church leaders. By the early 1940s Madeleva had long deplored the quality of religious education in Catholic schools, but it took a remark by her friend Frank Sheed about the fact that nowhere in the country could a layperson do graduate studies in theology to give her the idea that something practical might be done about the problem. And when her requests to Catholic University, Notre Dame, Marquette, and other universities to admit non-clerics to their graduate theology programs were turned down, she mentioned this disappointment to the head of the bishops' committee on the Confraternity of Christian Doctrine, Bishop Edwin O'Hara, while he was visiting Saint Mary's, and it was *he* who suggested that she might start something on her own campus. Mandell reports:

> At the time [Madeleva] demurred, fearful of what she described as "presumption." At the next meeting of the NCEA, with all other possibilities exhausted, she responded to "a strange impulse outside [her] will." Rising, she announced: "I do not know how we will do it, but this summer [1943] we will offer at Saint Mary's a six weeks' graduate program in Theology....We will send you details in a fortnight."[51]

[...] Saint Mary's School of Sacred Theology flourished for two decades, closing only when Madeleva's earlier goal of having university theology programs available to non-clerics had been achieved. During that time this small program prepared a generation of women theologians and has had an incalculable impact on the Church.

Having mentioned some of the contributions of Margaret Brennan, IHM, and Mary Anthony Wagner, OSB, we have only to reel in the chain of causality represented by another graduate, this one from 1954, to reinforce this point about influence. I refer to the theologian-turned-philosopher Mary Daly, who helped launch the Christian feminist movement and its theoretical contributions to Christian theology. If Daly had not earned her doctorate at Saint Mary's College, would she have been motivated to seek further training in Europe so that her theological knowledge would be certified with the same pontifical degree that clerical theologians possessed? Indeed, if she had not studied Thomas Aquinas so assiduously at Saint Mary's College, would she have been able to hold her own as the only female in a sea of cassocked seminarians at the University of Fribourg in Switzerland? We may well wonder whether *The Church and the Second Sex* would have been written and whether the discussion that ensued in Christian feminist theology would have been delayed or taken a different course.[52] The fact that Daly herself eventually rejected Catholicism and theology testifies to the ambiguous results of creativity but does not deny either Daly's or Madeleva's participation in culture-changing creativity.

I would note that the quality that led Madeleva to seek new solutions to significant problems can be called the virtue of creativity, insofar as a virtue is a moral excellence, a strength of character that contributes to habitually good action in some respect. As a virtue creativity involves the disposition to step back from a situation of difficulty, look at options imaginatively, and take reasonable risks for the sake of new and better possibilities. Creativity can, of course, be put to evil purposes, and in that case it is not virtuous.[53] And even when creativity is virtuous, its results will not be perfectly good, for under the conditions of finitude, human choices tend to have ambiguous results and unforeseen consequences. Furthermore, not every moral dilemma calls for a "new" response; discernment is needed to ascertain whether conformity or creativity is called for in a given situation, and often conformity is needed. For instance, when the Vatican insisted in the early 1980s that the Sisters of Mercy halt discussions in their hospitals about whether some sterilizations could be allowed, the women leading the community realized that failure to do so would likely cause division in the congregation and ultimately result in harm to their ministry of health care. Although the Mercy leaders did not agree with the Vatican's reasoning, they obeyed its demand for the sake of what they judged to be the greater good under the difficult circumstances they faced.[54]

For all these reasons it may be better to speak of the virtue of creative responsibility than simply creativity, for "creative responsibility" conveys the element of prudence, discernment, and caring as well as imagination. But however we name the quality, the important thing is to cultivate it. And I think we improve the odds of fostering this virtue if we think of moral education in terms of developing creatively responsible selves, rather than as a matter of "forming" some abstraction called "conscience." The investment of talents, whether one or two or five, must happen with the awareness that one cannot fully predict the results of a deed undertaken in the hope of doing good. But the Parable of the Talents from Matthew's Gospel makes clear that the willingness to take reasonable risks in responsibility before our Creator should characterize the person of faith.

MARY AS *LE POINT VIERGE*

Wendy M. Wright (2010)

The subtitle of this essay—*le point vierge*—I discovered first in the works of Thomas Merton, that ever-ready-to-explore-any-idea Trappist monk whose story and articulation of the monastic life so captured the imagination of the American public during the mid-twentieth century. Merton himself happened upon the provocative phrase in the writings of Islamic scholar Louis Massignon and immediately seized upon its poetic possibilities.[55] In his own turn, the older French scholar had been taken by the idea of *le point vierge* through his careful study of the tenth-century Sufi mystic of divine love, al-Hallaj, and continued to explore it after his own adult reconversion to the Roman Catholicism of his youth. So I follow the phrase back through this train of thinkers to the early medieval Islamic world. For al-Hallaj, the Sufi who was martyred for his more radical mystical statements, the *point vierge* was the secret place in the center of the human soul to which God alone has access. This virgin point, or as some have translated it, "virgin heart,"[56] was the goal of the Sufi mystical process of removing layers or veils from one's heart, a process accomplished through asceticism, meditation on the Qur'an, and acts of charity. The point of contact, beneath the seven layers of the heart, is *le point vierge*. Massignon for his part did Christianize the phrase and relate it to the long Marian tradition that viewed the Blessed Virgin as she was poised at the moment of the annunciation as humanity poised to receive the divine Word. But Massignon had a wider lens through which to interpret the phrase as well. Writing in the mid-twentieth century and riffing on this central teaching of al-Hallaj, the French Islamicist saw the need for cultivating a virgin heart as a prerequisite for interfaith encounter. What was needed, he believed, was a complete reversal of the attitudes toward other religions that were current at the time: what was essential was a radical hospitality in which the "Other" could be truly met. He specified that people get there by living according to *le point vierge*, that place of contact with God within each of us. Only when we live with and through the eyes of faith and love, which is what he means by living out of the virgin point, can we hope to understand the relationship of Christianity or Islam to God.[57]

From his cloister Thomas Merton carried on a lively correspondence with Louis Massignon. At some point, he became fascinated by the evocative phrase *le point vierge* and both spoke of it to his admired French correspondent and used it in his own writings. The ways Merton came to understand the phrase expanded its meaning. In one letter he referred to it as a sort of exhausted despair at the state of the world, the "virginal point, the center of the soul where despair corners the heart of the outsider."[58] This reading of the phrase is found in a series of 1960 missives to Massignon in which the Trappist reveals his anguish at the brutal violence evidenced in the French-Algerian conflict, an anguish shared by his correspondent. In another context but in a similar vein, Merton alludes to "the point vierge of the spirit, the center of our nothingness where, in apparent despair, one meets God—and is found completely in his mercy."[59] In yet another context the cloistered monk likened *le point vierge* to the temporal moment of passage from darkness to first daylight.

[…] Both a spiritual state, akin to the spark or apex of the soul to which the medieval Christian Rhineland mystics alluded, the location, as it were, of the ineffable encounter of human and divine from which all else has been emptied, as well as a state of created being where at the center of human nothingness one finds the Other, both the religious stranger and God, the virgin point seems to represent for Merton (as perhaps for the Sufi mystic and Massignon before him), liminality, the in-between-ness that returns us to the fresh possibility of re-creation as well as an apophatic experience that takes one to the very edge of the unsayable and unknowable. Mystical and political at one and the same time, the idea of *le point vierge* shimmers with numinous intensity.

I am aware that I run the risk of being grossly misunderstood in using the idea of the virgin point in my exploration of the figure of the Virgin Mary, even if I take it in a different direction than it may unfortunately often have been taken over the centuries in Catholic theology and spirituality. I am painfully aware that the concept of virginity, while a stunningly fruitful spiritual metaphor, has over the centuries been used oppressively to denigrate actual women and human sexuality in general. From the fifth century, when Augustine had to sort out the question of whether consecrated virgins who had been raped in the sack of Rome could still be considered qualified to claim their vowed state, to the centuries-long misogyny that stigmatized women as misbegotten males (who could overcome this only by overcoming their gendered identity), to the characterization of females as everything from "the devil's gateway" to the "weaker sex," to the dualism that has pitted Mary and Eve as symbols of good and bad females, to the persistent theological and pastoral denigration of marriage and sexual intimacy (identified with women), to the pervasive use of the Virgin to represent the sexless, obedient, good girl easily kept under control, to the "Marianismo" that extols the submissive, silent Latina who does not contest the machismo of her culture, the idea of Mary as Virgin has been sadly misused.

While I do not want to perpetuate these age-old sexist stereotypes and prejudices, I intend to be bold enough to hope that an expanded notion of the *point vierge* brought into conversation with the figure of the Virgin Mother may be enlivening and help us to think about her and ourselves in new ways.[60] For all she has led medieval armies and conquistadors into battle, for all she has served to shoo women religious back behind cloister walls, for as often as pious platitudes and vapid holy card images and narrowly conceived theologies may have imprisoned her, still I find a deep-down freshness, a liberating energy in Mary. It was Jesuit literary interpreter William Lynch, once again, who asserted in an essay he wrote in the mid-twentieth century for *Thought* magazine that "the primary goal of human life is the liberation of the imagination."[61] At this point I'd like to take him up on his challenge.

In the first place, I have been struck as I have walked my pilgrim road, with the almost dizzying variety of Marys I have seen and met. These multitudinous identities seem not to trouble most of the people with whom I have spoken. Although I have been appropriately cautioned by Marianist Fr. Johann Roten of the Marian Library at Dayton that all the Marys, whatever their visage or origin, must all remain identified with the scriptural Mary of Nazareth, and although Timothy Matovina has with compelling evidence claimed that devotion to Our Lady of Guadalupe cannot be described simply as an expression of Marian devotion, her role being too complex and her functions extending beyond those associated with Mary,[62] still I find her a central, powerful, and integrating symbol in the complex Catholic world. I have heard it said that Mary is such a rich, polyvalent, polyvocal symbol because of all the central symbols of Christianity, she is the least biblically well defined. That may be the case and that may provide her with sufficient flexibility to appeal to and respond to many different constituencies. Of course there are central Marian dogmas and a long tradition of Marian reflection, but these seem in practice simply to fold into the varied attributes and roles with which her faithful endow her. The tolerance for holding together in tension under one signifier—Mary—such a vast panoply of names, faces, qualities, capacities, and functions is a quintessentially Catholic one. In this sense, then, she is within the faith community a *point vierge*, a liminal, in-between reality where the diverse hopes and aspirations of many converge: a space where out of darkness hints of daylight begin to emerge. I see in her the dynamic, creative potential of the collective Catholic imagination that, while continually refining and clarifying itself through structures and doctrines, also refuses to be reduced to those clarifications. Alive, in-breaking, generous, and unpredictable, Mary waltzes back and forth from the center to the periphery of the tradition and back again, choreographing a dance into which all are invited.

According to Massignon, who opened his Catholic heart to the Islamic vision, and according to Merton, who so openheartedly met all those folks at the corner of Fourth and Walnut in Louisville, *le point vierge* is the place where the Other is truly encountered. This certainly has been my own experience on the Los Angeles pilgrimage road. I suspect this idea first came to me when I visited Our Lady of Peace in North Hills and heard the story of the parish deliberations that resulted in the creation of the multiracial fresco of Mary that serves to remind parish members that the Christian work of reconciliation and peacemaking begins in their intimate communities. My subsequent visit to Sacred Heart parish in Altadena, where the local Marian congress served to bring together constituencies that otherwise had little to do with one another, lingered with me. Mary as reconciling symbol not only expressed what people imaged and hoped for; she was also instrumental in bringing what was imagined into being. She became the mediating presence who facilitated an encounter with the strange and formidable Other. She became the common ground that enemies shared, the common ground of meeting and reconciliation.

Not only does Mary join communities of Others together, she has been at the virgin point of my own struggle to come into relationship with members of my own faith community who share little with me besides that affiliation. She has served as my own informal common ground undertaking. The polarized culture wars so painfully present in the American civil atmosphere are equally present in the American Catholic Church. I have found in Mary an entry point into the Catholic identity and the hearts of people on all ends of the ideological and theological spectrum. This has been important personal spiritual work. It has been good to seek to understand, to make sense of the motivations, the imaginative lenses, the anguish, and the hopes of those with whom I share a religious identity. It has also given me a glimpse of dawning, a new day, fresh with creativity and the possibility of renewed life.

But it is on another deeper level of encounter that in Los Angeles I discover Mary as the virgin point. There is something about the way my conversation partners describe their relationship to her, no matter what their perspectives on her or on life in general. There is a poignant tenderness, a palpable hopefulness that they communicate. There is no real reason why my interviewees should have been so forthcoming, so revealing of the depths of their love and longing in my presence except that their relationship to her is one of deep affection, and in me they recognized a similar love. They spoke not in a catechetical mode nor to impress or inform me but out of their deepest longing and most audacious hopes. Individual devotees may reject particular interpretations of Mary or be suspicious of other folks' way of perceiving her, but they all seem to have arrived at a suitable understanding that allows them access to an inner equanimity. She seems to represent, or even more provocatively to be present at, some deep, resilient space in the human heart in which newness and possibility germinate. I recall the voice of a sacristan in North Hollywood, a former actor whose near-death experience from drug abuse brought him back to his childhood faith, and the serene gaze of another volunteer parish worker in Paramount as he assured me that if you look to Mary, she will lead the way to her son, and the joy of two members of a Rosary group in Pasadena who recounted the relational healing that had taken place in families because Mary cared, or the deep trust of the mothers of the barrios who entrust their vulnerable children to *la Virgen* and find in her compassionate presence the strength to survive.

Once more, the words of Thomas Merton come to mind. Writing of contemplative prayer, his words capture something of my sense of this profound *point vierge* that I have sensed in the hearts of those who share their words about Mary with me. It is here that the analogical imagination opens out into the apophatic experience:

> In the "prayer of the heart" we seek first of all the deepest ground of our identity in God. We do not reason about dogmas of faith, or "the mysteries." We seek rather to gain

> a direct existential grasp, a personal experience of the deepest truths of life and faith, finding ourselves in God's truth.[63]

Beneath the veils that cover the heart, beneath our fears and views and ego-driven ideologies is a space, a virgin space not in the sense of absence of ambiguity nor pure because it denies the vagaries of the human heart with its cruel and destructive capabilities, but a space so deep and so poised at the edge of unknowing and the unsayable, that the outer layers that cover the heart are peeled away and yield to silence. A point where the stranger is encountered in the full mystery of otherness. A point where tensions meet and, not resolved, still create new possibilities. A threshold where the ultimate divine Other invites. At this point the heart breaks open and what remains is mercy, grace, forgiveness, reconciliation, hope, and beauty, beauty, and more beauty.[64]

Chapter 4
Gender and Sexuality

IMAGINING GOD, IMAGINING OURSELVES

Sandra M. Schneiders, IHM (1986)

In what has been said so far, I have attempted to locate with some accuracy the problem of the gender of God. The problem is not the sex of God (which does not exist) but our experience of God as masculine; and it is not the masculinity of Jesus (who is anything but a glorification of machismo) but his male sex. However, the reason Jesus's male sex is a problem is because it is seen as a revelatory confirmation of the masculinity of God and therefore of the divinity of maleness. Jesus, the man, is the incarnation of the Son of the Father. Consequently, our primary concern must be with the experienced masculinity of God.

God is not male; but we experience God as masculine. In other words, we imagine God anthropomorphically as male. There is a tendency, especially among those with a traditional Catholic education, to regard the imagination as frivolous, if not dangerous, capacity for nonsense in human beings who were intended to function rationally. In recent years the work of scholars in theology,[1] liturgy,[2] and scripture[3] has made us aware that the imagination is not primarily a reductive or combinatory faculty but is our constructive capacity to integrate our experience into dynamic and effective wholes which then function as the interpretive grids of further experience.

Perhaps our most accessible example of the functioning and the effect of the imagination is the formation of our own self-image. The self, like God and world, is not a finite and circumscribed entity of which we can take a mental photograph. To "get the picture" of ourselves is a never-ending process of integrating our experience into our sense of subjectivity in such a way that we can experience ourselves as other than and in some relationship to everything else.

The image of the self, like the image of God and of world, is not wholly the product of rational or deliberate processes but is a complex and dynamic reality which is formed by the interaction of conscious and unconscious factors in relation to actual experience. Once formed, the image organizes and interprets our experience so that what we actually experience as well as its meaning and significance is largely the function of our imagination. Thus, the person with a distorted self-image may be incapable of experiencing much to which she or he is actually exposed, may misinterpret what is experienced, and may draw all the wrong conclusions from it. The images of self, God, and world, furthermore, are incapable of total objectification and they are never static. We may know that our self-image is inflated, negative, or realistic, but we can never say exactly what our self-image is. Furthermore, our self-image undergoes constant modification as it interacts with our experience. In other words, the work of the imagination is ongoing. We are not the passive victims of our imaginations but can affect the vital images of self, God, and world.

It is important to recognize that the three basic life-structuring images—God, self, and world—are interrelated. If the world is imagined as a finite globe floating in space, God may well be imagined as a finite but very powerful being living someplace in space and acting upon the world. The self, in such an imagination, is a very small creature whose basic relationship with God is one of subjection to an all-powerful world-controller. In a world which is imagined as patriarchal in fact and by divine institution, God is necessarily imagined as the supreme patriarch. A woman with such an imagination must see herself as an inferior version of humanity subject first to human men and ultimately to the infinite divine male who established the patriarchal world order. This is, in fact, the imagination which the Church has gone to great lengths to encourage in both women and men. God is presented as a great patriarch whose enormous household is this world. This patriarchal father-God enjoys absolute and unaccountable power over nature and persons. This God recognizes in his male children a certain likeness to himself and places them in charge of his female children. However, in relationship to the divine patriarch himself all his children are feminine because, in relation to him, they are powerless and dependent.

The imagination is not entirely subject to rational control. Our God, self, and world images begin to form very early, and they are reinforced by our experiences at home, in school, in church, and in the broader society. These images carry such a numinous sense of reality that to interfere with them seems not only impossible but dangerous. To tamper with our images of self, God, and world threatens to destroy the very coordinates of reality. However, as we know, these images can be changed. World-images have been modified by science, by philosophy, by travel, by the arms race. And one of psychotherapy's major tasks is to heal the unhealthy self-image which paralyzes a person's capacity for life and growth.

The tenacity of the patriarchal God-image is such that many feminists have decided that the only course open to women whose self-image has been healed of gender inferiority and whose world-image has been healed of hierarchy is general and patriarchy in particular is to abandon the Christian God altogether. I would like to suggest that just as the self- and world-images can be healed, so can the God-image. It cannot be healed, however, by rational intervention alone. Repeating the theological truth that God is Spirit may correct our ideas, but a healthy spirituality requires a healing of the imagination which will allow us not only to think differently about God but to experience God differently. The imagination is accessible not primarily to abstract ideas but to language, images, interpersonal experience, symbolism, art—all the integrated approaches which appeal simultaneously to intellect, will, and feeling. What must be undertaken is a therapy of the religious imagination, first in regard to God and then in regard to our relationship with Jesus Christ.

[...] The maleness of Jesus is theologically, christologically, and sacramentally irrelevant. But the maleness of Jesus is definitely not irrelevant to contemporary spirituality. By spirituality I mean the lived experience of faith. It includes both how one relates to God and how one relates to self, others, and the world because of one's relationship to God. In this experiential sphere the maleness of Jesus presents a serious problem for women because the normative human being, the mediator between God and humanity, is irreducibly different from women. In a patriarchal society in which male superiority was accepted by women as well as by men this presented no problem. It made sense that God incarnate should belong to the superior half of the race and that women should be represented religiously, as they were in all other spheres, by a man. However, the fact that a problem did not exist in the past does not necessarily render it trivial or spurious. Just as earlier generations have had to wrestle with the Jewishness of Jesus, women today must wrestle with his masculinity.

Obviously, if Jesus was to be a genuine human being, he had to be either a man or a woman. The question for women is why he is a male rather than a female. We have already eliminated one reason, namely, that the God he incarnated was male. Now we must deal with a second widely held assumption, namely, that Jesus was male because God choose the superior form of humanity as the appropriate locus for divine self-revelation. The pattern of Old Testament revelation should long ago have put this male conceit to rest. God explicitly corrected a similar self-serving assumption on the part of the Jews, declaring: “It was not because you are more in number [that is, greater] than any other people that the Lord set his love upon you and chose you, for you were the fewest of all peoples” (Deut 7:7). And Paul applied the same divine logic to the earliest Christians:

> For consider your call...not many of you were wise according to worldly standards, not many were powerful, not many were of noble birth; but God chose what is foolish in the world to shame the wise, God chose what is weak in the world to shame the strong, God chose what is low

> and despised in the world, even things that are not, to bring to nothing things that are, so that no human being might boast in the presence of God. (1 Cor 1:26–29)

God's pattern is to choose the least suitable, the least powerful, the most shameful of human material as the locus for the divine activity in order to make clear that salvific action is truly God's.

It is clear that God did not become human as a man either because God is male or because maleness is divine. But we must still ask why, if female and male humanity are equally fitting material for the incarnation, male humanity was chosen. I would like to suggest that, in a certain sense, Jesus had to be a male in order to reveal effectively the true nature of God and of humanity.

First, Jesus revealed by his preaching and his life the inadequacy of the masculine definition of humanity. Jesus repudiated competition, the exercise of coercive power, all forms of domination and control of others, aggression, and violence. He espoused meekness and humility of heart, peacemaking, nonviolence, silent patience in the face of injustice and suffering, recourse to personal prayer in times of difficulty, purity of heart, and a nurturing concern for all, especially the sick, the oppressed, sinners, women, and children. In other words, Jesus delegitimized the stereotypically male "virtues" and the typically masculine approach to reality; he validated the stereotypically female virtues and lived a distinctly "feminine" lifestyle.

Had Jesus been a woman there would have been nothing revelatory about this way of life; women were expected to live and behave that way. Because he was a man, Jesus's choice of lifestyle stood out as a contradiction of the current definition of masculinity and thus of humanity as defined by the dominant male culture. But Jesus, choosing to live out a repudiation of the male value system, was recognized by friends and foes alike as possessing an arresting authority (e.g., Mk 1:28; Jn 11:48). So effective was his stereotypically feminine approach that he was perceived as a threat to both state and church. Thus Jesus undermined the accepted definition of humanity and challenged both men and women to conversion. He challenged men to abandon both their assumption of human superiority and the grounds upon which they based that claim. And he challenged women to value the traits which they had been taught to despise in themselves because they were despised by men.

Second, by his behavior and his teaching Jesus called for and inaugurated a reform of male-female relationships. Jesus chose women as disciples and apostles (cf. Jn 4:4–42; 20:11–18), taught women as he taught men (Lk 10:39), performed miracles for women (Lk 7:11–17; Mt 9:18–26), praised their faith (Mt 9:22), and accepted their love (Lk 7:37–38). At one point he seems to have allowed the superior religious vision of a Canaanite woman to broaden his own messianic self-understanding (Mt 15:21–28). Jesus defended women's loving service to himself and their ministry to others against the men who questioned, attacked, or belittled them (Mk 14:6–9; Jn 4:27–30). He rejected the reduction of women's worth to their reproductive functions when he corrected the woman who praised his mother for bearing and nursing him with the words, "Rather, blessed are those who hear the word of God and keep it" (Lk 11:27–28). He defended women against arbitrary divorce by invoking the order of creation in which the man as well as the woman was called to marital fidelity (cf. Mt 19:3–9). And he refused to collaborate in enforcing the sexual double standard by defending the woman taken in adultery whose partner in sin apparently had not been accused (Jn 7:53—8:11). Most amazing of all, the risen Jesus appeared first to his women disciples and entrusted to them the resurrection kerygma upon which the Church was founded (Jn 20:11–18; see also Mk 16:9 and Mt 28:9–10).

Jesus's attitude toward women was effectively revelatory precisely because he was a man in a culture which neither permitted nor rewarded egalitarian relations between men and women. The early church recognized as revelatory and acted upon the highly original vision of Jesus concerning the full personhood and equality of women. The question of whether women could be admitted to full Christian identity and mission through baptism seems never to have arisen despite the fact that there was no Jewish precedent for the religious initiation of women. The stories of Jesus's women disciples, even those stories in which Jesus took the side of women against men, in which women's fidelity concentrated sharply with the cowardice and betrayal of male disciples, and in which women have priority over men in the paschal events, were included in the Gospels. Women in the early Church were teachers and evangelists (cf. Acts 18:26), prophets (cf. Acts 21:9), and participants in public worship (1 Cor 11:5), and probably leaders of house churches (cf. Rom 16:1; Col 4:15).[4]

Despite patriarchal retrenchment and eventually male repression of women's participation in church leadership, the message of Jesus recorded in the New Testament remains a resource for women in their quest for justice and a clear condemnation of the men in the Church who have made void the word of God for the sake of their traditions. Today we would call Jesus a feminist, that is, a person who believes in the full personhood and equality of women and who acts to bring that belief to realization in society and the Church. It is hard to imagine how Jesus's challenge to revise the oppressive relations between women and men could have been presented by a woman. The most effective denunciation of injustice is that which comes from within the ranks of the oppressors. St. Paul says that Jesus was made sin for us (cf. Rom 8:3; 2 Cor 5:21). Part of the sinfulness he assumed was that of belonging to the oppressor class so as to act from within it to heal the division between men and women.

Third, Jesus definitively undermined patriarchy in a way that was open only to a male in Jesus's society. Although it is still oppressively active in the Church, patriarchy's days are numbered because Jesus destroyed its claim to be divinely instituted and sanctioned. As we have already seen, Jesus subverted patriarchy by his presentation of God as a nonpatriarchal father. But Jesus's personal choice of celibacy was an equally eloquent statement. In Jesus's society a man entered into the male privileged class by marrying and thereby becoming the head of a family. Jesus renounced participation in patriarchal privilege. He did not take possession of a woman and thus he remained free to relate to all women as equals. He did not have children, so he felt no need to dominate them and so teach them their place. Only as a man could Jesus repudiate patriarchy by his own choice not to legitimate it by participation.

The maleness of Jesus was certainly not an exaltation of masculinity or a revelation of the sex of God. On the contrary, Jesus accepted membership in the oppressor class of society in order, from within, to demonstrate the bankruptcy of the dominative social system. Only as a man could he have subverted the accepted definition of masculinity, validated the so-called feminine virtues despised by men but dear to God, redefined the relationship between women and men as one of equality and mutuality, and destroyed patriarchy's claims to divine sanction.

GOD'S PASSION FOR US

Elizabeth Dreyer (1989)

For Plato, the highest form of love is eminently rational, free from the disturbing influences of passion and sexuality. The object of this pure love is an impersonal ideal—Goodness itself. Love among humans has no place in this ethereal, idealized love. The primary difference in Christian love is that the object is no longer an impersonal ideal, but a personal God who is the fullness of love, in fact love itself.[5]

In Christianity, love of God is the primary love. Other persons and things are loved only as they reflect and lead to God. The experience of passion has been stripped of any bodily, material, human, sexual context and becomes the center of a purely spiritualized, mystical love. As mysticism is an extreme and intense form of religious experience, so it became appropriate for Christians to connect with it that intense form of affectivity, namely, passion.

Taken in itself, the connection established between mysticism and passion is a logical one. As we shall see, it set the scene for extraordinary religious experience and the literature describing it that is part of the glory of the Western Christian tradition. What is problematic for us today is any accompanying exclusion or denigration of matter, of human love, and especially of the passion associated with sexuality. While "passion" is not a four-letter word, its reputation has been tragically sullied.

Rosemary Haughton is one of few theologians who has grappled with these issues. Her books *The Passionate God* and *On Trying to Be Human* are examples of her attempt to take passion seriously and to explore its connections with the gospel message.[6] In general, Haughton defines "passion as the drive of powerful emotion toward the knowledge, and, in some sense, the possession of an object outside oneself."[7] The experience of passion can bring a sense of liberation from ordinary life, a profound increase in self-knowledge with its concomitant maturity, a renewed pattern of activity that perdures after the "feeling" of passion has passed, and a broadening of one's understanding of life beyond law and custom. All of this takes place in the context of relationship. The gospel calls us to be free to fall in love with other persons, and she regards the sexual expression of passion as the "type" of all passion because it contains within itself, by nature, the conditions for its own development toward wholeness and needs no help from outside.[8]

In *The Passionate God*, Haughton sets out to discover the radical implications of the poetic and scandalous statement that God became, and remains, human.[9] Only a love of intense passion on God's part can account for this gift to the world. With the incarnation and resurrection of Jesus as fulcra, Haughton builds a theology with the help of the concepts and language of the romantic love tradition. Central to this tradition are the ideas of "breakthrough" and "exchange."

According to Haughton, the paradigm of "breakthrough" is the incarnation in which the divine breaks into the sphere of the human. This breakthrough has several consequences. One of the most important is that it makes nonsense of the division of reality into material and spiritual. Second, incarnation does not affect only human beings but "involves every level of reality from the most basic particles to the ultimate Being of God."[10] The incarnation makes holy all materiality and bodiliness.

Haughton further suggests that the medieval category of "being" rings in the modern ear as a static concept. It has what she calls a "stopped" quality. Therefore, she prefers to talk about the totality of life in terms of "love" rather than in terms of "being" since love implies dynamic relationship. Love cannot be love unless it is given and received, that is, "exchanged."[11] This exchange goes on everywhere, from the intimate recesses of the Trinity to the lowliest form of matter.

For Haughton, the language of romantic passion provides the kinds of "concepts, images and language tools which can enable us to articulate the theology of exchange."[12] The images of passion, she says, are images of love in action pointing to some kind of breakthrough to an encounter that is perceived as difficult.[13] It is not too difficult for us to imagine the person of Jesus, walking the earth in his gentle, determined, healing way. Nor is it difficult for most of us to imagine deity as infinitely loving creator of the universe. It may not even be hard for us to imagine the persons in the Trinity in some kind of close relationship. But a totally unimaginable oneness, a divine passion so intense that God *has* to be Jesus and a Jesus so passionate he *has* to be God—this is "so outrageous a demand on human intellect and human courage that there are only two possible responses: utter faith or utter rejection."[14]

Haughton writes about the passion God has for human persons. This divine love works for, in, through, and between people, embracing the "entire, mysterious and infinitely complex system of interrelationships which is creation."[15] In particular, she believes that we can gain some insight into the passion that drove God to become incarnate by looking carefully at the way people love people, especially as that love is passionate "because that kind of love tells us things about how love operates which we could not otherwise know."[16]

But in spite of this creative theological analysis of passion, questions about the role of passion perdure. Is it possible for us to benefit from learning about the passionate love of the mystics? Is it possible to rehabilitate sexual passion in a Christian context, to envision a harmony between intense sexual experience and the rest of one's life—including one's commitment to Christianity? Because passion is dangerous—and few would deny this—must it be banished from the realm?

Some persons react negatively to attempts to recover passion, fearing a loss of reason and an ensuing chaos. While it is a truism that one must be ever vigilant to protect reason, I think that in the west we have erred in the opposite direction. I search theological literature to find warnings about the sins of the intellect to match the seeming terror aroused by sins of feeling and passion! However, we do indeed need to guard against an understanding of affectivity that is narrowly sentimental, falsely grounded in an illusory dream world, maudlin, or egotistically romantic.[17]

But is it possible to broaden the horizons of our understanding of passion? What are the ways in which the presence of passion can enhance one's existence? One takes it for granted that passion drives great warriors, poets, and lovers. Is passion the exclusive domain of such persons? Are such persons possessed of a certain personality structure that lends itself to living a life of intensity? Or can "passion" be understood on other levels so that ordinary people might expect and be open to the ways in which passion can be life-enhancing? For example, how might the presence of passion change our experience of marriage, learning, appreciation for nature, child-rearing, attitudes toward injustice? Might we ever arrive at the point at which a life devoid of passion, like the unreflected life, is a life not worth living?

JOB AND THE SITUATION OF WOMEN

Joan Chittister, OSB (1990)

The classic parable of affliction, the book of Job, traces a history of suffering and a concept of power that may well provide a model for understanding the situation of women in our own day and for dealing with it as well.[18]

There is an element of the book of Job which, I think, warrants special notice. Job, you see, is not a Jew. It is Job, the Gentile, the figure outside the system, who confronts it with the reality of undeserved pain.[19] It is Job, the innocent one, who brings Israel to deal with its own notion of God and life and the theology of sin and suffering. The situation fills a reader with tension. How shall we account for the wanton oppression of whole classes of people—slaves, blacks, women—while others for reasons just as capricious live lives that are self-determined and free of arbitrary controls or groundless suffering. The book of Job confronts us with a dilemma as contemporary as it is overwhelming. Job's suffering is not the plan of God or the will of God or the test of God. It is not God, after all, who is afflicting Job. It is the Accuser who questions Job's endurance and Job's abilities and Job's fidelity.[20] It is the Accuser who sets out to try Job. It is the Accuser who changes Job's life and cuts off Job's opportunities and holds Job in servitude to sorrow. What is to be thought about this? What is to be learned from this by the poor of today's world, by the forgotten of today's world, by the women of today's world?

In Job, too, even the friends of the oppressed blame the victim. It is the reasonable and the orthodox who claim that this suffering is God's will for Job. It is the pious who insist that Job deserves the suffering and will be saved by the suffering and should be glad for the suffering. It is the faithful who insist that Job's plight must have something to do with infidelity. But Job insists on asking why such a thing can be. And Job wants to know the cause of the opprobrium. And Job rails against the suffering and the answers that are given to it. And Job challenges the world to prove that it is indeed God who has done this thing. And Job wants to know the why of it all. It is Job who says, "I have prepared my defense and I know I am right."[21]

"You are undermining religion and crippling faith in God," Eliphaz the Temanite says. The advice is clear: Don't question your fate. Don't challenge it. Don't resist it. Be docile, in other words. Be obedient, in other words. Accept your proper role in life, in other words.

"We are old. We speak with the wisdom of age," Eliphaz argues. "It's always been this way, in other words. This is clear and constant tradition you are fooling with. This is the custom of time immemorial. What has made you so wild that you spew your anger at God and spit out such insolent words?"[22]

Sin. Tradition. Wisdom. Obedience. The natural law. God's will. Every argument in the lexicon of the comfortable, the powerful, the pious is used against Job. But Job will not relent. Job demands more than formula faith. Job demands justice. "Enough," Job says. "I have heard enough! I am sick of your consolations. I too could say such things if you were in my position: I could bury you with accusation and sneer at you in my piety or whisper my easy comfort and encourage you with a word."[23] Job's rage has no bounds now. "O earth, do not cover my blood. Never let my cry be buried," he screams.[24] Clearly, there are some things that simply cannot be accepted. There are some things too inhuman for a human being to accept. There are some things that no amount of virtue can absorb without risking the greatest unvirtue of them all, injustice.

Then, not surprisingly, even Job's faith in God begins to waver. Job's love for humanity begins to wither. Job's hope in everything he once thought good begins to pale.

Be obedient, Zophar cautions. Listen to the plan for you.

You are morally inadequate, Eliphaz argues. Realize your condition. God knows I am innocent, Job counters, and God knows that those worse than I reap the graces of the land.[25] "Be humble," the friends insist. "Then God will bless you."[26] Be silent. Be satisfied. Be nothing. And be it all in the name of God.

But Job's strength is stubbornness. Job's power is the unassailability of powerlessness. What else does Job have to lose—except, of course, his integrity, his identity, his self. "I will never let you convict me," he insists. "I will never give up my claim," he promises, though in recognizing his condition and railing against the groundlessness of it all, Job has lost prestige and honor and the social place.[27] "Now I am their fool....They stand beside me and sneer....They rush at me in a mob....And now I am in agony," Job laments.[28] To assail the system, Job discovers, is no small task, no reasonable discussion, no simple process. Whatever ideas or creeds or classes the system systematizes are not to be tampered with, not even in the face of the obvious.

Yet to take justice unto himself, to allow his anger to destroy him, to become what he hates, Job learns from God, is no solution either. Job's hope is in God alone. Job's salvation lies in being able to see with new eyes. Job's hope does not rest in avenging the old system but in beginning to envision a new one. Job's transformation lies in being able to distinguish between the designs of God and the destructiveness of evil operating in the name of God. Job's salvation lies in using power well.

Indeed, the cry of Job through history has been a long, long wail.

It has been the wail of Jews on their way to the ovens, struck down by those who claimed the power of God.

It has been the wail of Cambodians in labor camps, struck down by those who claimed the power of God.

It has been the wail of refugees on the West Bank, struck down by those who claimed the power of God.

It has been the wail of dayworkers and the unemployed and the displaced, all struck down by those who claimed the power of God.

It has been the wail of all the forgotten masses of the world.

And today, in our time, Job is a woman.

Job, this voice of universal suffering, fits the female picture all too perfectly: Job was a person faithful to God and compassionate with people. Job had a family and raised them to be true. Job lived responsibly and quietly and piously. Job was gentle and nonviolent and trusting. But when Job was afflicted, when Job cried foul, all the weight of the system fell upon his back. Rather than lift the burden from his body, the system condemned Job for his complaint. And Job was told that this senseless degradation was the certain, the conscious, the unending will of God for him.

But in the last chapter of Job, finally, the sacred writer puts before us one of the most challenging developments in scripture.[29] Those friends and observers of Job's who took upon themselves the task of declaring Job's sufferings to be the will of God for him are humbled. Those who lied about God for the love of God must give tribute, God insists, to the very one they rushed with their unholy use of power. Finally, those orthodox friends of Job's, so smug in their righteousness, so certain in their attitudes, so secure in their superiority, so insistent on the unchangeableness of their brand of orthodoxy, are confronted with the profoundly unorthodox. In Job's world, after the scourges are over, when the accusations have ceased and the wrongs have been righted and Job has found that it was not God who was unjust to him and God has found Job to be true, a shocking transformation occurs. Now, in this world where things are finally right, only Job's daughters, not Job's sons, are named—Dove, Cinnamon, and Eye Shadow, the translators call them—and the feminine is allotted an unheard-of equal share of the family inheritance.[30]

In this new world where God's will is no longer thwarted, in other words, those struck down are raised up, the feminine is valued, oppressive power is disempowered so that the powerless can triumph, the relationships of the world are reordered, and hope is made new in Job's daughters. In this new vision, Job sets the feminine free. Job uses his power to eliminate the divisions that put people in contention. Job uses his power to make his world whole.

Indeed, Job is a story of power gone awry: the Accuser, the friends, the society all claim that Job is Job's problem, that Job is inherently inadequate and deserving of his state, that in Job's nature itself lies the fault of his own suffering, that Job is deficient, morally deformed, spiritually inadequate, that Job deserves what Job is getting, that God has ordained it so, and that salvation for Job depends on humble acquiescence.

Job's story is, indeed, the story of any woman in the world today who suffers the arbitrary judgment of femaleness, who bears oppression in her own body, who is faithful to God and is told that God is the reason for her suffering, who has known what it is to have people blame the victim, who asks questions and is called heretic for the asking, and whose future is in her daughters as well as in her sons.

Job's friends use ideology, office, and law against him, too. They blame the victim, they remind him of his status in life, they claim that his suffering is due him, they insist that all the degradation is the will of God for him. Women recognize all the theory.

Women, too, have been taught that if they are raped and beaten, it is their own fault. They have been taught that they are intellectually, emotionally, and morally inferior to men. They have been taught that suffering is their lot in life. They have been taught that God favors men but not women. They have been taught that God is male and that, therefore, males are closer to God.

They have been taught, like Job, to accept their lot without question. They have been taught that questions are heretical.

They have learned best what the theorists have only speculated about: power indeed profits the powerful. Those who occupy society's positions and interpret its ideologies and write its laws have power. Those who do not, do not. Women have been taught to believe that things as they are, are things that are good for them so that they will endorse their own oppression and maintain the powerful in power unimpeded.

And, like Job, they are questioning, contending, rebelling. Everywhere.

[...] What is threatening about the woman's movement is not that the woman's movement is changing the domestic role of women. What is threatening about the woman's movement is that it challenges the very foundations upon which power is based in every institution in society.

Like Job, women know that the inhuman and the unequal and the unfair simply cannot be the will of God.

Like Job, who confronted God to discover the reason for his suffering only to find out that there was no reason, feminist theologians and philosophers and biologists and psychologists are confronting the systems that restrain them only to discover that there is no real reason for the disempowerment of women across the world except the disempowering power structures of men.

And, like Job, women know that things must be changed if God is going to be allowed to be God.

The symbol of Job's new world is the symbol of Job's three daughters—Dove, Cinnamon, and Eye Shadow, the translators call them—not invisible now but named, not dependent but propertied, not faceless but uniquely gentle, personable, and female. In Job's new world, the feminine is very present and just as powerful, just as established, just as influential as her brothers are. Job's new world, in other words, is the world turned upside down. In this world, equality does not diminish resources, it doubles them. In this world, the development of women does not diminish men, it enhances them. In this world, conflict is not the basis of security and peace and feminism does not signal weakness; it secures the strength of everyone.

That world is yet to come for women.

THE RELATIONALITY OF SEXUALITY

Lisa Sowle Cahill (1992)

Catholic revisionist thought about sexuality often or even typically reacts against what can only be described as a "pre–Vatican II" mindset in which sexual morality was defined in terms of procreative acts in marriage. The narrowness of this vision and the scrupulosity and guilt it perpetrated among Catholics certainly deserve to be repudiated. However, Catholics born during or after the council no longer have the same need for "liberation" from a repressive sexual ethos.

If we consider the current North American cultural ambience, then reassurances to young adults like "Sex is good—a simple statement and yet one often disputed" or "Despite our negative experience, the Christian conviction stands: the body is holy; sex is good; God dwells here"[31] seem not only anachronistic but irrelevant. Young Catholics are confronting a culture in which "value-free" encouragements to sexual enjoyment, combined with peer pressure to trade sex for status, leave a trail of confusion about how to formulate any sexual norms at all which go beyond individual preference and free consent. While pre–Vatican II Catholics needed to discover intimacy in order to transcend the biological/functional, procreation-centered view of sex within Catholic culture, post–Vatican II Catholics need to recover both intimacy and the parental potential of sex in order to offset the sex drive/individualist, gratification, centered view of it. Just as surely as did the older model, but in an opposite way, this newer cultural ethos overwhelms the sense that sex is personal and relational.

It is in its affirmation that sexual union, psychological and emotional intimacy, and shared parenthood are interdependent and mutually reinforcing realities that Catholicism has a message for our broader cultural ethic of sexuality. The necessary correction to the traditional way of stating this unity is to add that the three "Catholic" values of sex, love, and procreation are all to be understood as ongoing personal relationships rather than as isolated acts or qualities of acts. And, as against common cultural assumptions, these relationships are not three essentially separable "options" but are intrinsically interconnected. Catholicism's prophetic ideal—that personal commitment, sexual expression, and shared parental creativity are mutually integral ongoing relationships—does not yield a simple new code of specific sexual behavior. Ideals for sexuality, as for other spheres of moral relationship, must be translated into practical reality with prudence and sensitivity to the limits of the human condition. However, the prophetic ideal should always inform evaluative thinking about sexual conduct and relationships and should somehow be operative in specific conclusions.

[...] Sex is fundamentally and above all a relational capacity, and the relationships it implies include not only the sexual partners but also children, family, and society. The relationships among physical sex, personal partnership, and parenthood as the outcome of sex form a moral unity, and in this unity consists the moral meaning of sexuality. "Reproduction" is not a capacity which can be understood apart from the context of human sexuality as relational vis-à-vis both the child and the co-parent. The relationality of sex is fulfilled most perfectly in the parenthood of spouses, situated within an intergenerational family network which opens out onto and participates in the common good of the community as a whole.

To conclude, women's experience of sexuality, given both its biological and its historical contours, should well attune us to the potential of sex to be *parental*—not in the narrow sense of "procreation" but in the sense of an ongoing social bond of nurturance and love: Our experience of sexuality also includes a sense of its power for intimacy and union, grounding shared family life. These values are not values only for women. But women can affirm their value for men on the basis of what has already been their greater realization in women's lives. Women's sexuality can be a window onto the elemental meanings of human sexuality: it finds its meaning through the mutuality of partners in sexual desire and fulfillment; in the durable, intimate friendship enhanced by "tenderness" (Ricœur); and in the arduous but delightful procreativity of sex, an avenue for mother and father to share "attentive love" and care (Ruddick), a love as bounteous in human meaning as the sexual and spousal bond.

ON MOTHERING

Diana Hayes (1995)

Black women have borne many trials and tribulations in Western society. Yet there has always been that "something" that has enabled them to continue "to rise." Alice Walker credits Jean Toomer with articulating that unexpressed something that often the women themselves were unconscious of. She states:

> When the poet Jean Toomer walked through the South in the early twenties, he discovered a curious thing: black women whose spirituality was so internal, so deep, so *unconscious*, that they were themselves unaware of the richness they held.[32]

She continues:

> They dreamed dreams that no one knew—not even themselves, in any coherent fashion—and saw visions no one could understand.
>
> They wandered or sat about the countryside moaning lullabies to ghosts, and drawing the mother of Christ in charcoal on courthouse walls.
>
> They forced their minds to desert their bodies and their striving spirits sought to rise, like frail whirlwinds from the hard red clay.
>
> Our mothers and grandmothers, some of them: moving to music not yet written. And they waited.
>
> They waited for a day when the unknown thing that was in them would be made known; but guessed, somehow in their darkness, that on the day of their revelation, they would be long dead....

> For these grandmothers and mothers of ours were not saints, but artists; driven to a numb and bleeding madness by the springs of creativity in them for which there was no release. They were creators, who lived lives of spiritual waste, because they were so rich in spirituality—which is the basis of art—that the strain of enduring their unused and unwanted talent drove them insane.[33]

They sought not merely a "room of one's own" in which to write, to be free, to create and be, in turn, re-created; they sought and were too often denied a life of their own, a being, a freedom which was of their own making and owed nothing to the false largess of a master or mistress or, sometimes, even, of a husband. I think of Rebecca Jackson who, when called to serve as God's minister, despite the protestations of family, husband, and church [male] ministers, "left her husband and her brother's house…[to] become an itinerant minister who found fellowship (more accurately 'sistership') among other black women who organized 'praying bands.'"[34] An illiterate woman required to ask her brother to write letters for her only to discover that he was putting his own words in, Jackson was "taught to read and write by the spirit within her":

> One day I was sitting finishing a dress in haste and in prayer. This word was spoken in my mind, "Who learned the first man on earth?" "Why, God." "He is unchangeable, and if He learned the first man to read, He can learn you." I laid down my dress, picked up my Bible, ran upstairs, opened it, and kneeled down with it pressed to my heart, prayed earnestly to Almighty God if it was consisting to His holy will, to learn me to read his holy word. And when I looked on the word, I began to read and when I found I was reading, I was frightened—then I could not read another word. I closed my eyes again in prayer and then opened my eyes, began to read. So I done, until I read the whole chapter.[35]

How did they do it, we ask? How did they manage to keep their creativity alive year after year and century after century, when for most of the years Black people have been in America, it was a punishable crime for a Black person to read or write? And the freedom to paint, to sculpt, to expand their mind with actions of any kind simply did not exist.[36]

How did they do it? How did they continue to sing, to pray, to sew quilts worthy of hanging in exalted museums throughout this land? How did they do it—and, more importantly, how did they pass it on—to me and to my sisters, those before and those coming after me?

[...] Bernice Johnson Reagon speaks in terms of "mothering"—a term not limited, however, just to those women who have actually given birth to children. For her, the understanding of a mothering generation encompasses "the way the entire community organizes daily to nurture itself and its future generations." She speaks of women who

> were the heads of their communities, the keepers of the tradition. The lives of these women were defined by their culture, the needs of their communities, and the people they served. Their lives are available to us today because they accepted the responsibility when the opportunity was offered—when they were chosen. There is the element of transformation in all of their work. Building communities within societies that enslaved Africans, they and their people had to exist in, at least, dual realities. These women, however, became central to evolving the structures for resolving areas of conflict and maintaining, sometimes creating, an identity that was independent of a society organized to exploit natural resources, people, and land.[37]

Mothering thus requires an ability and willingness to maintain traditions while reshaping them for future generations—discarding that which is not nurturing and upholding while incorporating that which is. Mothering reveals the many ways "a culture evolves and how and why changes occur in order to maintain the existence of a people."

Reagon affirms that

> within the story of the African diaspora, there is the opportunity to see a process of continuance and transformation at work among women cultural workers. Their struggle to contend with a new space entails defining their people and children in new ways. That definition disrupted and threw into severe trauma cultural practices that had been nursed in African societies. Mothering, therefore, required a kind of nourishing that would both provide food and stamina for survival within a cruel slave society and the passing on of traditions that would allow for the development of a community that was not only of but also beyond the slave society. These women had to take what they were given from their mothers and fathers (for as she notes, mothering is not limited just to women) and make up a few things. Nurturing was not only reconciling what was passed down to them with day-to-day reality but also sifting and transforming this experience to feed this child, unborn, this new Afro-American community, in preparation for what it would face.[38]

It is this understanding or concept of "mothering" that is a critical aspect of womanist ways of being in the United States today. It is by the continuous telling, despite the obstacles set in one's path, of "the history of one's people to future generations," thereby "imparting cultural values to the children of those generations, [that] Black women throughout the diaspora have kept their heritage" [and as a result] the Black community alive and intact.[39]

These mothers, grandmothers, and co-mothers, aunts and play aunts, older sisters and godmothers formed a community of women that renewed community and sustained the spirit in its midst.

The Black Church has, historically, been the source of community life in all its variations—social, economic and cultural. Ironically, Black women, although the foundation of the Church, have not played significant leadership roles therein, although not for lack of trying. As Jacquelyn Grant asserted in 1979, Black women are indeed the backbone of the Church, but for too long the emphasis has been on "back" as in the background—out of sight—called forth only when needed—for Women's Day or other fundraising events, to clean the church or to cook for and take care of the male ministers. The failure, Grant asserts, "of the Black Church and Black Theology to proclaim explicitly the liberation of Black women indicates that they cannot claim to be agents of divine liberation."[40]

Fortunately, many Black women have taken to heart Sojourner Truth's words, given at the 1852 National Women's Suffrage Convention: "If the first woman God ever made was strong enough to turn the world upside down all alone; together women ought to be able to turn it right-side up again."[41]

Thus, "through the necessity of confronting and surviving racial (and sexual) oppression," oppressions joined in all too often by those who should have been their natural allies, Black men and white women, "Black women have assumed responsibilities atypical of those assigned to white women under Western patriarchy."[42]

Casting aside the myth of "True Womanhood," a myth they were never allowed to participate in fully, at any rate, Black women have forged new ways of being in the world which, in keeping with Alice Walker's terminology, they name as "womanist." They have done so because it was a necessary part of proclaiming who they were as women and as Black in a world and society which places little value on either status.

[...] Black women are the "mothers," the bearers of African American culture. They must speak for themselves because no one else is able or willing to speak for them, nor are they willing any longer to be spoken for. They have gone back to their spiritual roots in Africa and the United States, recalling the spirits of those women of "stout step" and strong fists to discover, recover, and reproclaim the African ethos which nurtured and sustained them from generation to generation down through the ages.

They have looked within themselves and their Black sisters to find that spirit of God which has always been with them but which, over the years of their sojourn in this strange land, they have, at times, lost contact with. They look to the writings of Black women, writings which affirm Black culture and Black community for their ways of seeing and of being are "alternative" rather than "oppositional":

> Much of African-American (male) literature has been oppositional, since the focus of the works tends to be on articulation of self as opposed to white men/white society. But the women may tell another story. Like their spiritual foremother Hurston, the African-American (female) writers demonstrate that documenting alternative cultural practices may open up other ways of seeing which have been lost both in opposition to and in competition by the dominant culture. One might say that the writings themselves are part of an alternative cultural practice, challenging the "canon" of African-American literature and criticism—and the practice is both residual and emergent. This alternative practice does not pose Afrocentric against Eurocentric binary oppositions; rather, it exposes some of the hidden modes of African-American community ties which have transformed both African retentions and Euro-American realities into a way of survival.[43]

This way of "mothering" is one in which womanists are also engaged recognizing that

> as long as the Black struggle refuses to recognize and deal with its sexism, the idea that women will receive justice from that struggle alone will never work....In the words of Sekou Touré: "If African women cannot possibly conduct their struggle in isolation from the struggle that our people wage for African liberation, African freedom, conversely, is not effective, unless it brings about the liberation of African women."[44]

Liberation cannot be partial or in stages. A womanist is one who is "committed to the survival and wholeness of an entire people, male *and* female. Not a separatist, except periodically, for health. Traditionally universalist...."[45] This means that the struggle for liberation must be one that encompasses race, class and gender—at all levels, for all peoples. For, as Fannie Lou Hamer succinctly put it: "How can I hate another human being and expect to see God?"

BIRTHING THE SACRED

Sidney Callahan (2003)

Now I can see that religious experience, even the most intense religious experiences of hearing voices and seeing visions, can be the happy result of innate human cognitive predispositions of our embodied and socially embedded human nature. Evolutionary developments of the brain and body produce readiness for both concrete and transcendent experiences of others and of the More beyond. Reductive materialistic views of religion as pathology or wish fulfillment have not won the day. Today it is possible for secular psychology to provide evidence that human beings are innately ready and responsive to God and God's call. What skeptics read as irrational pathological projection upon reality can be convincingly seen as the reality of God-readiness in the human race. How I wish that I had known more about the sources of religious experience during my earlier bouts of self-doubt! Knowing more about the depths of the human mind and heart could have helped me accept the reality of my own powerful experiences of God's loving presence. A fuller understanding of differential diagnosis and the discernment of spirits could have reassured me.

Of course it is also of vital interest to note that the original primary dialogue that begets the self and the sense of the sacred is with a woman. Does this reassessment of the birth of the sacred have any bearings on our understanding of women's religious experience?

A defense of the validity of religious experience basically applies to both men and women despite the fact that religious women have been more subject to reductionist dismissals. Still, the question can arise of whether women have unique features and characteristics in their religious experience. Such a question about gender can stir up a hornet's nest in and out of religious thought. Many feminist thinkers emphasize how much alike men and women are (equality feminists), while others wish to focus on differences or essential differences between the genders (difference feminists or romantic feminists). Those who advocate the notion of essential gender differences will want to find unique feminine characteristics in women's religious experiences, since women's special gifts must be uniquely their own and celebrated as such. Womanly insights into God and religious truth should speak to us in special and penetrating ways through time. Women who are equal in the sight of God will still give glory to God through their essential nature and in the complementary relationship to males.[46]

I am of the feminist persuasion that emphasizes how alike men and women are in their mental, moral, and spiritual capacities. I judge the evidence of both psychology and Christian theology to show that differences among individuals are not so much the result of gender but are more usually caused by the multitude of other individual differences that always exist among persons. Individual differences have more importance than gender differences. Individuals are more themselves in their particular constitutions, personalities, and moral choices than they are like other women or other men of the same gender.[47] Gender differences will be minor compared to other characteristics. Individuals qua individuals will be shaped by their innate intellectual, emotional, and temperamental characteristics, interacting with their individual actions within the historical cultural conditions within which they live and operate.[48] Genes are crucial, but there are a lot of them that are not associated with gender. And experience, like genes, can change the brain and body.

[...] Given the evolutionary and cultural history of women in the Christian West, I think we could hazard some tentative generalities about women's religious experiences. While equality feminists can be correct in stressing the primary importance of individual characteristics, other gender universals may play a part. If it is true that the mother-child relationship is the primary interpersonal bond affecting human development and marks the genesis of both the self and a sense of the sacred, then women have been greatly favored by evolution in their reproductive and nurturing potentialities for positive creativity. No wonder there have been so many mother goddesses in human history. Women's enabling power arises from their ability to create new life and sustain family kin groups. By internalizing maternal images young women may be more disposed to developing psychological nurturing and to creating caring relationships.

Women's traditional roles may have made them ready to receive the gospel good news of God's loving care for humankind. Christianity gained many converts among women because of the appeal of its basic messages about the value of human life and the importance of women's roles in the family.[49] Women's embeddedness in embodiment and interpersonal emotional experience would make them appreciate the incarnation and its validation of the body. Moreover, if personal relationships are the ultimate reality of God as Trinity, women's concrete experiences of constantly being in relationship would prepare them for community life in the Church. Love of every kind, familial and erotic, must always have played a large part in female lives and socialization, so it is not surprising to find women using these images to express their love of God and God's love for creatures. While males could resonate to ideas of Jesus as mother, women would find them particularly convincing.[50] Women must also have appreciated the practice of speaking of the Holy Spirit as feminine.

The knowledge that the Holy Spirit freely inspires women outside of the Church's hierarchical channels ensures that women could have an important role in prophecy and the life of the Church. Women's association with the Spirit's freedom combined with women's long association with children can also account for female mystics' use of childlike and playful imagery, a practice that so offended proponents of religious gravitas and seriousness. Fortunately, a lack of official social roles in the Church and the world can have its compensations; women have been freer to be emotional, playful and take risks in their religious experience. Women can dare to be thought mad or neurotic or excessively emotional, like lovers and children. Has not Jesus pointed to great lovers and to the child as the way to the kingdom? The gospels have always validated the worth and great happiness granted to those who are poor in spirit, those who hunger and thirst, or mourn. Those who seek with the most fervor will be most open to being filled and will be the most grateful. Women for all of the above reasons may be open to the Spirit and consequently be gifted with joys and blessings.

So too, women's religious experience has often been prophetic in anticipating and moving the Church forward to a fuller understanding of God's maternal mercies toward all. Women's openness to emotional religious experience, especially in intense forms of mystical manifestations, has borne fruit in wisdom. Ron Hansen, a novelist writing on the history of the stigmata, has noted that "women are seven times more likely than men to get the stigmata"; he speculates that this disproportion may "be God's way of illustrating the importance of women in Christ's ministry and of correcting the imbalance in Holy Scripture, where a far higher proportion of men have their voices heard."[51] From a theological perspective one can affirm that women's religious experience has been a strategic work of the Spirit in the world.

Women who hear voices and see visions and have prophetic and intimate religious experiences have given witness to God's justice and equality while affirming God's maternal love. As in the past, so into the future. Christian women gain authority in the Church and the world through their Spirit-filled religious experiences. This is right, good, and fitting for a religion that begins with one woman's belief in God's good word to her. Mary tests her angelic experience by asking how this can be, but, being satisfied in her discernment, she places her complete trust in God. Mary's faith in her experience of God's bestowal of love ensures the salvation of the world.

WOUNDED HEALERS

Mercy Amba Oduyoye (2018)

Bernadette Mbuy-Beya, a religious sister and a member of the Circle [of Concerned African Women Theologians], reflecting on the Circle's understanding regarding HIV/AIDS, concluded that "the lack of women's rights has killed more women than any physical malady." We may not have the relevant statistics to back all this, but we speak and theologize out of experience, and we know that God does not approve of senseless, needless suffering of creation, human or otherwise, man or woman. And that is why Denise M. Ackermann, in "From Mere Existence to Tenacious Endurance Stigma: HIV/AIDS and Feminist Theory and Praxis," opines that "theologians have to engage the messiness of life by trying to nurture gospel practices in the midst of tribulation."[52]

African women theologians live out of a spirituality that flows from their own life experiences and urges them into the type of praxis that Ackermann writes about. Fulata Moyo's experience is that "the telling of painful stories helps us embark on the process of narrative theology for health."[53] She therefore includes stories and the reflections upon them as healing when utilized as "counselling services to guide prayer casualties back to spiritual wholeness and health." Many struggle with unanswered prayers, especially those who are told it is their own lack of faith that prevented the answers from reaching them. Women's healing services in the context of this spiritual struggle are summed up in Fulata's offering, which says, "Relating unanswered prayers to lack of faith is untheological, as it creates unnecessary guilt on the part of care-givers." We struggle with how our caregiving can be anchored on a "sense of God's will for life." Nonetheless, women are moved to continue caregiving of many types while they themselves continue to seek God's will, so they may say with Ackermann that those who pray "May your kingdom come" remain conscious that "it requires the willingness of those who pray this prayer to translate it into deeds."[54]

Hajia Katumi Mahama's contribution to *Women in Religion and Culture: Essays in Honour of Constance Buchanan* highlights, in her contribution on "Empowering Muslim Women for the Third Millennium," the truism that

> the problems of disease, poverty and war affect women and children most when they occur. This is enough to urge women, irrespective of their religious affiliation, to close ranks and join hands in finding solutions to the problems that affect all women. To achieve maximum success, the co-operation of men and women is greatly needed because the issue is one which affects both men and women.[55]

The Circle's interest in health and healing shows its concern for human rights. It is the right of God's creation, including humanity, to live what God saw and pronounced good in the pristine state of creation. God will not apply "good" to a diseased body. Jesus was obvious in his pro-health stance, and so the women in this lecture see health as a human right and as a result participate in healing ventures, as well as in attempts to prevent what violates the growth of healthy conditions. Concern for healthy relations between women and men is linked with the violation of the human rights of women.

Healing in the Circle involves participation in advocacy for healthcare delivery. Most of what we have done as the Circle is exemplified in our advocacy for care of people infected and affected with HIV and AIDS, and the elimination of stigmatization in relation to the pandemic. Our educational events around HTPs [harmful traditional practices] are endeavors toward advocacy for transformation or elimination as deemed appropriate. Though our forte has been research, writing, and public education, some of us have been and continue to be involved in prison ministry and in soliciting for materials for hospitals and hospices. We have not been healers only, but also women who have been healed and continue to crave healing. The two women whose research was used in the section on deliverance ministry have themselves undergone deliverance.

In all of this, we have anchored our faith on the "theology of hope," as found in several of the offerings, but especially in Denise Ackermann and Fulata Moyo. With Fulata's "Eschatological Hope as Healing,"[56] I conclude my effort to survey women theologians' contribution to health and healing. The burden of her essay is on guiding "prayer casualties" back to spiritual wholeness and health. The challenge of unanswered prayers and unanswered questions remains dire for those who seek health, healing, and wholeness. Fulata opines that the telling of painful stories helps us embark on the process of "narrative therapy" for health. She offers healing as a notion of eschatological hope.[57] When seeking health through medicine seems to fail us, we resort to health care through miraculous cures. It is in this regard that the place of faith becomes a two-edged sword. Healing depends on the faith of the healer and that of the one needing to be healed. When it does not happen according to the prayers and rituals, the conclusion is lack of faith in one or the other. Fulata narrates her experience when her husband, Solomon, was diagnosed with liver cancer. In his last days, he announced, "I want to go home." Fulata knew that she needed "the encouragement and solidarity of other Christians...with Faith for healing to stand against the inevitable." She offers us the notion of healing "as eschatological hope" that "promises us new beginnings in which new life is discerned dualistically."

Fulata sees Solomon's new life in death as influencing the life of his earthly family through their memories of him as their ancestor. "For the bereaved his new life also affirms hope for new beginnings in our calling and mission to transform the world."[58] The experience of the passing of Solomon has taught new meanings and new expressions for us to discern why God's answer may contradict our own. Our task as caregivers should therefore include creating safe spaces for the expression of emotional frustration to God and to those who are accompanying us in our quest for therapy. Our theology of hope is anchored in God's unconditional love, God's justice, and God's infinite wisdom, as God intervenes in our lives and seeks out the best in a situation.

We saw how Landman focused on counseling. Fulata regrets "the lack of professional counselling services in most Christian communities." She goes on to say that "prayers offered in times of disease are seldom pastorally or theologically guided towards spiritual wholeness and health." She points to the common explanation of "failed prayers," "You needed more faith," as contradicting the very nature of God's love and God's preferential option for the oppressed. She opines that "the emphasis on believing faith on the part of the intercessor as prerequisite to divine healing unnecessarily fabricates accusations about its lack, in the face of supposedly unanswered answers creates unnecessary guilt on the part of the caregiver on top of the usual grief caused by so many unanswered questions."

She suggests that making available sensitive pastoral care that deliberately involves the patient in decision-making instead of the "imposition of prayers or words of encouragement" would help even caregivers to hope for "eschatology that begins now." If we had allowed Solomon to decide what type of prayers to be offered and when, what course would his six-week period of illness have taken? Could it be that he wanted to have the serenity of his own sense of God's will about his life? Was he tired of us forcing our concept of healing into his life? I sometimes wonder.[59]

I have presented Fulata's experience in such detail to underline the Circle's emphasis on experience and on its method of narrative theology. African women are wounded healers, and their own words should be heard. These have been the words of my sisters in the Circle, and my hope is that it can bring health and healing to healers and readers.

Reflecting on all these, I offer my understanding of healing as mending broken relations, in individuals, between persons, and in the community's self-understanding. I have not looked at the Christian theology of reconciliation, which deals with mending relations between individuals and God and between God and humanity in general. I have not looked at healing as redemption though the concept, together with salvation, liberation, and deliverance, is related to restoring well-being at various levels. The object of healing in this offering should provide the groundwork for mending broken nature. We are living with a cracked earth and abused nature, and this situation, too, calls for healing. The ecological crisis cries out for healing in terms of getting rid of the anthropocentrism that gives humans the impunity to rape nature, so we can overcome our propensity for abusing the earth. Mending broken relations between races, ethnic groups, and faith communities, and embracing the existence of diverse sexual orientations, calls for establishing mutuality and recognizing the joy in the rich diversity of humanity. As Christians, a good deal of our quest for healing depends on healing biblical hermeneutics, while Muslims do the same with their sacred scriptures, and as Africans, our quest is for healing our cultural hermeneutics. As African women theologians, all these challenges of interpreting our triple heritage are before us as we attempt the multifaceted task of healing and promoting health living. Current popular preaching that tends toward literal appropriation of biblical events and concepts, if not curbed, will soon be justifying slavery, as it already justifies sexism and family codes that are misogynistic because they are androcentric.

SALVATION IN THE SHADOW OF FEMINICIDE

Nancy Pineda-Madrid (2019)

Even though salvation is of unparalleled importance to the Catholic Church and its theology, the Church has never officially adopted a single formulation of the doctrine of salvation. Of course, there are primary commitments that distinguish a Catholic understanding of salvation: principally, that Jesus the Christ is the mediator of salvation and that all human beings need salvation, claims without which we would not be speaking of a Christian understanding of salvation. Still, the Christian tradition across its two-thousand-year history has been receptive to pluralism in its understanding of salvation, recognizing the wide range of "human existential reality."[60] Such invites the endeavor to seek out a credible understanding of salvation in the shadow of feminicide.

Moreover, my pursuit of a credible understanding of salvation begins with a foundation of five guiding assertions that clear a space for the particular understanding of Christian salvation that then follows. The work of both Roger Haight, SJ, and Josiah Royce significantly informs my thinking in all that follows.

The *first* guiding assertion is that God reveals Godself in human history, in liberating historical events. Accordingly, salvation is rightly understood as something we experience, at least in part, in the here and now, in history, rather than exclusively in the afterlife. The in-breaking of the kingdom of God[61] in history, the intensification of God's grace in human history is the work of salvation. Consequentially, salvation is, to some degree, realized in history. Even so, this realization is not the whole of salvation, which only comes in the fullness of time, in eternity. As the unique and whole revelation of God, Jesus actively worked to realize the kingdom of God in history, ongoing work that the Holy Spirit continues into our own time and beyond. The ongoing saving work of Jesus is always in history.[62]

The in-breaking of the kingdom of God in history is the work of salvation, yet this in-breaking never occurs in the midst of a benign reality. Rather, it always takes place in the midst of the anti-Kingdom, that is, the coalescence of various death-dealing forces that vitiate what God has created. Work on behalf of the kingdom of God always "brings out the reality of the historical anti-Kingdom."[63] Indeed, the coming of the kingdom of God, as Sobrino exhorts, necessitates a struggle against and "a triumph over the anti-Kingdom."[64]

The historical endeavor to subvert the evil of feminicide is work on behalf of the kingdom of God and is work of great complexity. The victims of feminicide must remain a dangerous memory for all disciples of Christ, haunting us so that we forge a world where feminicide is no more. "It is not those innocent of evil who are fullest of the life of God, but those who in their own case have experienced the triumph over evil."[65] Indeed, salvation can only be realized in a world in which it is in question. Thus, while we can never entirely rid the world of evil, we can subordinate and subvert it. We partially realize salvation in history when we seek the greatest good through the subordination of evil, which entails a critique of and a dismantling of death-dealing ideologies. However, when we experience evil, that is, when we suffer, particularly when we suffer unjustly, our initial inclination tends to be to destroy the source of our suffering, which is often another human being. Most often good and evil are bound up together such that the destruction of evil would destroy good as well. The human who responds by destroying does not realize the greater good, while the human who, having suffered, uses her or his suffering creatively toward some greater purpose allows all to glimpse a vision of the spiritual ascendancy of the good in history.[66] How we come to terms with what we have already suffered (past tense) is as crucial as our efforts to subvert the ills we can foresee.

The *second* guiding assertion affirms salvation as God's revelation. Salvation entails "a reconciliation between God and human existence"[67] that comes about through God's incessant, loving presence in our midst. Through God's self-communication with us, God constantly seeks the renewal and deepening of union with human beings: this is salvation. Jesus uniquely and fully reveals God's constant presence and ardent desire for communion with human beings and with all of creation. Yet there is more. Jesus's lifelong practice of loving us continuously actualizes our communion with God, making this communion ever more visible and relevant.

Salvation as revelation includes the whole of creation. Augustine and Aquinas, among many other theologians, have recognized that the whole of the natural world is revelatory of God, that it is the second book of revelation.[68] As Elizabeth Johnson has taught us, creation has three dimensions: (1) *creatio originalis* (the original gift of life given by God to plants and animals); (2) *creatio continua* (God's sustaining presence to plants and animals without which they would cease to exist); (3) *creatio nova* (God draws and renews all of creation by opening up new possibilities for the future).[69] These three dimensions of creation show us something of God's benevolence, capaciousness, and gratuitousness; and these dimensions beckon us into a deeper relationship with God, with one another, and with the whole of creation. This movement is salvific.

What is being revealed by God is the fundamental spiritual unity of the world. God's Spirit continuously draws and lures us all into communion with God, with all humanity, and with all that is in and of the world, indeed, every being in creation. It is supercommunion writ large. Evil utterly obscures this communion, attempts to destroy any sense of communion, and diverts human attention away from God's revelation. Accordingly, salvation in the shadow of feminicide must account for the most extreme, utter affront to the fundamental spiritual unity and communion that God wills for the world.[70]

The *third* guiding assertion is that salvation is nonsensical when it is *exclusively* reduced to a personal, individual concern. When understood as narrowly a personal, individual concern, our understanding of "salvation" slips into a kind of theological solipsism. This line of thinking implies a god who is uninterested in the human community as such and is only interested in individual lives. Certainly, this is not the God of Jesus Christ, not the God of Pentecost, not the God of the New Testament, and not the God of the Jews in the Hebrew Scriptures (Old Testament). While always personal and individual, salvation inevitably concerns the social givenness of human existence and beyond. Moreover, salvation as a personal, individual concern is nonsensical because, as Haight points out,

> Human existence is a social phenomenon, so that even the individual, in his or her quasi-autonomy, is at the same time a function of social relationships, not to mention intrinsic, organic relationships with the world of nature. This anthropology of human solidarity describes an ontological condition; these relationships constitute persons whether or not they are always explicitly aware of their formational character.[71]

And, because "human existence is a social phenomenon," a social metaphysics can ground and contribute to a cogent Christian understanding of salvation. A social metaphysics is a way of understanding reality that takes our interrelatedness with all other human beings, all other creatures, and all that has being as fundamental to our self-understanding. If we hold that the nature, constitution, and structure of reality is fundamentally social, then we must recognize that this line of reasoning bears theological and soteriological significance, not only for the human community but also beyond as well.

Further, a social metaphysics implies a consciousness. Individual human consciousness and a social consciousness have meaning and value only in light of a larger unity of consciousness. "The whole reality of the universe itself must be defined in terms of the reality of such an inclusive and direct grasp of the whole sense of things."[72] All of humanity, nature, and creation is to be included in the grasp of the whole. This larger unity of consciousness is a transcendent consciousness, a superhuman consciousness. This transcendent consciousness that constantly interrelates all that has being may be called the Interpreter Spirit, the immanent divine active in the world, God.[73]

To understand Christian salvation in the shadow of feminicide requires foregrounding of the human capacity to actively recognize the social constitution of human existence and actively participate in the transformation of the underlying social structures that fuel the possibility of feminicide and that are heinously sinful. If human beings remain passive or blind to the social structures and mechanisms that shape our lives, then religious discourse about salvation will appear unintelligible if not irrelevant.[74]

The *fourth* guiding assertion is that salvation is *integral* in nature, meaning that it takes into account the whole of life, every dimension of life without exception. "Salvation is an all-encompassing concept that reaches out toward integrated human wholeness."[75] This is another way of saying that salvation understood in exclusively spiritual terms cannot respond to the evil of feminicide in any credible way. Arguably, salvation narrowly focused on the spiritual, at best offers a deficient understanding of salvation regardless of one's life circumstances.

If salvation is understood as the realization of wholeness and integration in the most exhaustive sense, thus on an individual and social level, then it is best understood as coming about through processes of interpretation, that is, processes of interpretation that achieve two ends. First, these processes increase the visibility of the inherent interrelatedness of all humans and all creation. Second, these processes seek out the meaning of this interrelated vision in the face of the fragmentariness and brokenness that eventually marks all life. Interpretation here is understood, above all else, as a process of integration happening on many levels and, accordingly, not exclusively on a cognitive level. It is a process that is also affective, physical, kinesthetic, and so forth. Again, the all-encompassing integral nature of salvation is the work of the Spirit of God active in the world, animating every inclination toward human integration (personal and social) and every inclination toward recognition of the interconnectedness of all that has being.

Salvation in the shadow of feminicide must account for the extreme difference between the world as it is—one in which feminicide occurs—and the world as God desires the world to be, that is, a loving, reconciled world. Indeed, religious language about salvation must confront all that is an utter affront to what God wills for the world, in this case, the affront of feminicide. The traumatic wounds left in the wake of feminicide make the notion of a possible reconciled world seem utterly monstrous, absurd, impossible, and literally unimaginable. Here we confront the limits of human imagination. In the wake of extreme evil, how might human wholeness be advanced? Are there individuals and communities who have experienced extreme evil and yet, through their coming to terms with this experience, suggest to the rest of us a path forward, a path toward healing and integration, even more toward wholeness? Again, "It is not those innocent of evil who are fullest of the life of God, but those who in their own case have experienced the triumph over evil."[76]

The *fifth* and final guiding assertion is that salvation "in our world must address the connection between human action and the ultimate state of things, the eschaton," as Haight has argued.[77] How does human action, particularly collective human action, orient us, or not, toward the question of ultimate meaning, toward what is of ultimate value? In our time, a growing number of people have a heightened awareness of how social systems and structures privilege certain groups of individuals and marginalize other groups. Further, while evil human action has been part of the human story since the beginning of the human race, today our capacity to extend the impact of evil human action is greater than it has ever been, owing to a myriad of human scientific and technological advances. Human beings use these advances for great good and great evil.

Too often we blind ourselves to the great evil that is being done to the most vulnerable; we blind ourselves by creating a circumscribed worldview in which we distance ourselves from serious and widespread innocent suffering outside of our particular sphere.[78] Far too often, the question of meaning and value is engaged on the basis of a reduced sphere of concern and *not* on the basis of meaning and value on a global and ultimate scale. As a result, the question of *ultimate* meaning and value, because it always includes the whole interconnected world and the whole of human history, is not embraced, much less addressed. When this happens, we cling to a distorted understanding of salvation, so much so that we end up no longer talking about a Christian vision of salvation.

To be sure, salvation in the shadow of feminicide must take seriously the question of *ultimate* meaning and value. To the degree that Christians remain passive in the face of unjust social structures that make the eruption of feminicide more likely, or remain blind to what is beyond their own circumscribed world, to this degree Christians' consciousness and freedom will become attenuated and submerged. Injustices beyond their personal experiences become more of an abstraction than a reality. As a result, disciples often become less desirous of and zealous for the fullness of justice, goodness, and truth in this world and lose sight of the eschaton. Passivity or blindness to what lies beyond our particular world precipitates an obscuring of the gospel vision of the kingdom of God that Jesus Christ devoted his whole life to announcing and actualizing, a vision that provoked his crucifixion.

Chapter 5
Culture and Dialogue

FROM DUALISM TO KINSHIP

Elizabeth A. Johnson, CSJ (1993)

I am persuaded of the truth of ecofeminism's insight that analysis of the ecological crisis does not get to the heart of the matter until it sees the connection between exploitation of the earth and the sexist definition and treatment of women.[1] As a theologian I am further convinced that the distortion found in those two instances also influences the Christian experience and doctrine of the mystery of God. This, I suggest, is the genius of women's spirituality in our day, informed by feminist analysis: that it sees the deficient pattern as a whole rather than in bits and pieces. Having faced something of the devastating result, let us cut to a major taproot of the crisis, namely, the dominant form of Western rationality called hierarchical dualism.

This is a pattern of thought and action that (1) divides reality into two separate and opposing spheres, and (2) assigns a higher value to one of them. In terms of the three basic relations that shape an ecological ethic, this results in a view in which humanity is detached from and more important than nature; man is separate from and more valuable than woman; God is disconnected from the world, utterly and simply transcendent over it, as well as more significant than it. Hierarchical dualism delivers a two-tiered vision of reality that privileges the elite half of a pair and subordinates the other, which is thought to have little or no intrinsic value of its own but exists only to be of use to the higher.

In the form in which it affects Christian theology and most of Western thought, hierarchical dualism was first articulated in ancient Greek philosophy. Here it is envisioned that reality is composed of two separate levels of existence, namely, spirit and matter. Spirit is a transcendent principle that brings into play activity, autonomy, reason, the mind, the intellectual, the soul, the permanent, the infinite. Matter, on the other hand, is the principle signifying immanence, which shows itself in passivity, dependence, emotions, the body, the physical, nature, the transitory, the finite.

In some ancient conceptual frameworks matter and spirit thus distinguished exist in a harmonious tension of opposites. But the thought pattern that became most influential in subsequent tradition separated and graded them. Consequently, rather than existing in dialectical interplay, these two spheres of existence are described as polar opposites and their differences are maximized. With a logic that assumes differences automatically signal the presence of something inferior, spirit and matter are also ranked. Spirit is valued more highly than matter, which, as a lower, entrapping element, is meant to be controlled for the sake of spirit. These two aspects of reality, in other words, are separate and unequal.

The resulting dichotomy is familiar to anyone educated in Western anthropology. The essential self is the soul, which is divided from the body. In the resulting hierarchy of the self, the body is less valued and is even given a negative connotation, while the mind is prized as more permanent, closer to the sphere of divinity, and meant to rule over the recalcitrant flesh.

Feminist reflection brings to the fore another basic element in this construction, namely, that it equates spirit with the masculine principle in the world while matter is identified with the feminine. In terms of actual people, this means that men are linked with a transcendent, spiritual principle beyond nature, while women and the earth embody the lower, material principle, existing with a natural inferiority for which there is no remedy. The hierarchy of mind over body in the individual is therefore not a neutral construction but has political consequences. It translates into social structures of domination/subordination undergirded by the belief that man should rule over woman, the quintessential "Other" whose reproductive power and survival skills he needs and gets but whom he is also free to disparage. This arrangement does not benefit all men, but only those of the ruling classes. Onto other men of the lower classes and different races are also projected the same so-called feminine qualities of bodiliness, irrationality, and so forth that cry out for "stronger" male control. "According to Aristotle's *Politics*, ruling class Greek males are the natural exemplars of mind or reason, while women, slaves and barbarians are the naturally servile people who must be subdued and ruled by their 'head.'"[2]

This social dualism in the human community, thought to be naturally in tune with the shape of the universe, also has ecological consequences. For the earth is matter, the antithesis of spirit. The ruling man's hierarchy over women and slaves extends also to nature, most often symbolized as female. She is meant for his service while he, in his nobility, has a duty and right to tame and control her. The female symbolism for nature that generally pervades human thought arises from the fact that women are the life-givers to every human child, as the earth itself, Mother Earth, brings forth fruits. Within a system of dualism, however, both women and the natural world are separated from the men they bring forth and sustain. Both are assigned instrumental value, with little or no intrinsic worth apart from their potential to serve the needs and desires of men. Women whose bodies mediate physical existence to humanity thus become symbolically the oldest archetype of the connection between social domination and the domination of nature.

[. . .] The influence of this massive heritage sheds some light on the peculiar neglect of God the Holy Spirit in Western Christianity. The whole Church remembers the Spirit on the feast of Pentecost and on the occasion of the sacrament of confirmation; charismatic Christians pray and heal in the power of the Spirit; and local communities may invoke the Spirit before making important decisions, singing the ninth-century hymn "Veni Creator Spiritus," "Come, Creator Spirit." But apart from these instances there is little sustained appreciation of the Spirit in an existential or intellectual way. As Heribert Mühlen observes, when most of us say God, the

Holy Spirit never comes immediately to mind; rather, the Spirit seems like an edifying appendage to the doctrine of God.[3] In unusually colorful language, theologians today describe the Spirit as the forgotten God, something faceless, shadowy, ghostly, vague, the poor relation in the Trinity, the unknown or half-known God, even the Cinderella of theology.[4]

The logic of hierarchical dualism sheds light on why this is the case. Valuing spirit over body and transcendence over immanence, it concentrates on the one high God who creates by "His" word to the neglect of the indwelling, sustaining presence of God within the fragility of matter and historical process. When this pattern of thought turns to trinitarian theology it keeps the focus on the relation of Father and Son, one generating and the other being generated, finding it difficult even to know what proper name to give the Spirit. Dualism has trouble with threes.

But it is not only the framework on which the doctrine of God is built that excludes the Spirit. In a subtle way this mindset connects the Spirit with the female side of the dualistic equation, with women's reality and functions, which it disvalues. The Spirit brings forth and nurtures life, keeps all things connected, and constantly renews what the ravages of time and sin break down. This is surely analogous to traditional "women's work" that goes on continuously in home and society, bringing forth life, holding all things together, cleaning what has been messed up, while unnoticed and unremunerated. Neglect of the Spirit has a symbolic affinity with the marginalization of women and is an inevitable outcome of a sexist, dualistic lens on reality, which also, let us remember, disvalues nature.

The extent of what is lost to the richness of faith can be glimpsed when we realize that what is being neglected is nothing less than the mystery of God's personal engagement with the world in its history of love and disaster; nothing less than God's empowering presence active within the cosmos from the beginning, throughout history and to the end, calling forth life and freedom. Forgetting the Spirit is ignoring not a faceless, shadowy, third hypostasis but the mystery of God vivifying the world, closer to us than we are to ourselves, drawing near and passing by in liberating compassion.

Three basic relationships: human beings with nature, among themselves, and with God. In each instance the major classical pattern of relationship is shaped by hierarchical dualism, that is, modeled on the dominance of ruling male elites and the subjugation of what is identified as female, cosmic, or foreign, an underclass with only instrumental value. As the ecological crisis makes crystal clear, the polarization of each pair's terms is nothing short of disastrous in its interconnected effects. Our eyes have been blinded to the sacredness of the earth, which is linked to the exclusion of women from the sphere of the sacred, which is tied to focus on a monarchical, patriarchal idea of God and a consequent forgetting of the Creator Spirit, the Life-giver who is intimately related to the earth.

In the quest for an ecological ethic grounded in religious truth, these three relationships need to be rethought together. But we must be wary of roads that lead to dead ends. I think it is a strategic mistake to retain the dualistic way of thinking and hope to make an advance simply by assigning greater value to the repressed "feminine" side of the polarity. This is to keep women, earth, and Spirit in their preassigned box, which is a cramped, subordinate place. Even if what has previously been disparaged is now highly appreciated, this strategy does not allow for the fullest flourishing of what is confined to one pole by preassigned definition. In truth, women are not any closer to nature than men are; this is a cultural construct. In truth, women are every bit as rational as men, every bit as courageous, every bit as capable of initiative. At the same time, precisely because women have been so identified with nature, our voices at this moment in time can speak out for the value of despised matter, bodies, and nature even as we assert that women's rational and spiritual capacities are equal to those of men. What we search for is a way to undercut the dualism and to construct a new, wholistic design for all of reality built on appreciation of difference in a genuine community. We seek a unifying vision that does not stratify what is distinct into superior-inferior layers but reconciles them in relationships of mutuality. Let us then listen to women's wisdom, discern our kinship with the earth, and remember the Spirit, as vital steps toward an ecological ethic and spirituality.

[...] If separation is not the ideal but connection is; if dualism is not the ideal but the relational embrace of diversity is; if hierarchy is not the ideal but mutuality is; then the kinship model more closely approximates reality. It sees human beings and the earth with all its creatures intrinsically related as companions in a community of life. Because we are all mutually interconnected, the flourishing or damaging of one ultimately affects all. This kinship attitude does not measure differences on a scale of higher or lower ontological dignity but appreciates them as integral elements in the robust thriving of the whole.

Take, for example, trees. Their process of photosynthesis creates oxygen, the most essential, life-sustaining element in the air we breathe. Without trees there would be no animal or human life on this earth; we would all be asphyxiated. Now, biologically speaking, trees do not need human stewardship. Without human beings they existed very well for millennia. Human beings, however, positively need trees in order to breathe. Who, then, needs whom more? By what standard do human beings say that they are more important than trees? At this point in evolutionary history, we form one mutually interdependent community of life. We are all kin.

WHAT COMPASSION ADDS TO CARE

Margaret Farley, RSM (2002)

What "compassion" adds to "care" conceptually is both an element of stronger affective response and an assumption of more acute access to knowledge of the concrete reality of others. If care is the affective response to persons in need, compassion is this same response with the added notion of "suffering with" the ones in need. We all know the reasonable and necessary cautions to caregivers about not being inordinately "emotionally involved" with those for whom they care.[5] We also know the factors and forces that prevent "suffering with"—noncompliance on the part of patients; ingratitude; even the apparent repulsiveness of some patients; and the fatigue, impatience, weakness, and humanly limited generosity of spirit of all caregivers at one time or another. Yet at the heart of the various medical professions there lies not only the possibility but the vocation to some degree and some form of compassion. From the vantage point of compassion, we can better understand the mutual relationship and inseparability of compassion and respect, justice and care, principles and persons, autonomy and beneficence.

Precisely because compassion involves a beholding of the value of others and a suffering with them in their need, it opens reality to the beholder; it offers a way of "seeing" that evokes a moral response. The suffering of others is one of the locations in human experience where, whatever our epistemological skepticisms, we do encounter the reality of others and ourselves.[6] Perhaps nowhere is this more evident than in the clinical context of medicine. Here the needs of persons are frequently dramatic. Sometimes they rival any affliction known to human persons. Bodies are consumed by pain and disease; minds and spirits, too, are assaulted by loneliness, fear, and despair. Long nights and days go by where the endurance of patients, families, and caregivers is tested. Infants and young women, old men and strapping athletes, the injured and the ill dwell in a world of waiting or a world in which the favored medical metaphor is battle for life and for health.

Other kinds of suffering and need also dwell in the spheres of struggle and hope that characterize human life. There is the kind that does clearly lead to new life, literally to birth, or to new strength and mobility, new forging of family ties, new hope in a shared future. There is the kind where, out of disaster, injury, unexpected crushing disease, the battle is won, the unexpected ensues, the sorrow and pain yield to joy and comfort all around.

The point is that suffering in some form, great or small, overwhelming or overcome, has the power to grasp us when we see it in others. It has the power to hold us so that we cannot avoid the reality of the sufferers or the reality of ourselves. Insofar as we genuinely behold it, it awakens in us a moral response—to alleviate it, ameliorate it, prevent it in others, or if none of this is possible, to companion and literally "bear with" the sufferer in love and respect.

In the medical setting, not all suffering is paradigmatic in this way. But even when it is not like this, the response to persons in need frequently derives from or participates in our perception of dramatic needs. If we cannot always see so clearly the concrete reality of each patient, or if we do not respond affectively in every situation, we nonetheless draw analogies from our deepest experiences and our most penetrating insights.

To behold, or even to remember, acute suffering can, of course, just as well distance us from one another, dull our moral sensibilities and the acuity of our ethical discernment. Moreover, if care can be mistaken, sometimes it is because our perception and interpretation of suffering is false. Compassion gives us access to concrete reality, and it awakens in us a moral response, but respect, too, can sharpen the focus of what we see and keep our compassionate responses fitting and true.

Compassion and respect are, therefore, mutually illuminating, and together they constitute a way of seeing the concrete reality of those who are in need. Compassion sheds light on the individual patient in her concrete situation in all of its particularity and complex embodiment; it also illumines the situation of sickness, reveals the form of relationship needed between caregiver and patient, places in relief structural deficiencies in the providing of care. It is not blind to the vulnerability of need, the asymmetry of caregiving relationships, the ways in which freedom is for the sake of relationship, but relationship makes freedom possible. So, too, the norms of respect, in the affirmation of the well-being of others and ourselves, shed light on what compassion will require: the maximization of autonomy insofar as possible, the protection of bodily integrity in some significant sense, the provision of knowledge and competent care, fidelity to commitments, honor to personal stories and deeply human hopes.

Compassionate respect, compassionate justice—here is a framework for an ethics of medical practice that, while moving beyond the dualities of other frameworks and approaches, does so responsibly only by incorporating them in a structured discernment for response. It moves beyond the polarities of care and autonomy, care and justice, persons and principles by allowing the content of respect to provide the criteria of care—by, that is, requiring care to be respectful of embodied autonomy as well as every level of need in the person to whom care is owed.

BEAUTY ENLARGES THE HEART

Susan A. Ross (2006)

"Love your neighbor as yourself" is one of the "two great commandments" (Mt 22:39), yet there has been a strong theme in the Christian tradition that self-love is potentially something very dangerous. One of the earliest challenges to traditional Christian understandings of love, sin, and grace was Valerie Saiving's essay in the *Journal of Religion* in 1960, when she suggested that the root of sinfulness in human beings might not be, as Reinhold Niebuhr suggested, in too much pride and self-love, a too large ego and self-centeredness, but rather in its opposite: that women too often had a lack of self-love and, too often, put others before themselves. Since then, many others have picked up on this theme, and it has become one of the most well-developed ideas in feminist theology.[7]

The significance of self-love has not been a theme only for feminists; a number of Christian theologians have developed it in recent years.[8] This emphasis on self-love has accompanied an emphasis on mutuality, a theme that has also been taken up by many thinkers, both those who would identify themselves primarily as feminists and those who would not.[9] It is worth noting that Thomas Aquinas argued strongly against loving one's neighbor more than oneself.[10] I would like to pick up on the themes that have been developed by feminist theologians surrounding love of self and mutuality and suggest a connection with beauty and generosity.

In order to do this, I turn to the ideas of Elaine Scarry, as she has developed them in her book *On Beauty and Being Just*, and those of some other recent writers on beauty.[11] In her book, Scarry develops a theory of beauty and identifies some key features of beauty. These are, first, that beauty is sacred; second, that beauty is unprecedented; third, that beauty is lifesaving; and fourth, that beauty incites deliberation.[12] She summarizes these features at one point by remarking: "Something beautiful fills the mind and yet invites the search for something beyond itself, something larger or something of the same scale with which it needs to be brought into relation."[13]

Similar ideas are developed by other writers on the topic of beauty. Frederick Turner, in his book *Beauty: The Value of Values*, mentions the sense of recognition that accompanies a sense of beauty, and its inexhaustibility and depth.[14] He also comments that "[b]eauty can almost be defined as an absence of the desire for power, possession, success, political victory in themselves" and continues by noting that "there is a 'giving-away' in beauty, a sense of nothing to lose."[15] David Bentley Hart includes beauty's objectivity, its ability to cross boundaries, and its freedom.[16] All of these authors point to a certain fluidity in beauty, while it is, at the same time, quite particular.

A very loose and preliminary definition of beauty would be that of a kind of ordering of material, intentional or not (as in nature), in a way that presents a unique vision or sensory experience of some dimension of the experienced world that gives the beholder both pleasure and a sense of deeper meaning.[17] I would emphasize my qualified use of such terms as ordering and vision. By order, I do not mean to refer to some idea of hierarchical order (although this may be involved) but to something more along the lines of an arrangement that is somehow pleasing. And by vision, I do not intend to indicate only visual beauty and to exclude music or tactile beauty but rather to refer to the completeness of the presentation as it is experienced by the beholder.

The authors I have mentioned here, and many others, describe an excess that is characteristic of beauty: what is truly beautiful cannot be put into a careful formula, nor can it be adequately described. And beyond beauty's inexpressibility is what Scarry describes as beauty's quality of "greeting": "At the moment one comes into the presence of something beautiful, it greets you."[18]

There is, I suggest, an intrinsic generosity that is characteristic of beauty. Real beauty does not exclude; rather, it invites. Real beauty does not "count up" but rather flings its gifts to anyone who asks. Real beauty invites exploration and depth; it does not shut the door prematurely to the questioner. Beauty is always ready to give more. When we encounter a beautiful work of art, we find ourselves unable to exhaust fully the beauty that it offers. When does one get tired of great works of art, of sunrises and sunsets, of gardens, of our loved one?

Such generosity is one of the main ways in which Jesus describes God: as the father of the prodigal son who welcomes him back without condition and throws a huge party; the vineyard owner who pays everyone a full day's wage, even those who only worked an hour or two; the God whose love is so immense that this God is with us in our very flesh. Much of what has been traditionally taught in Christian ethics has emphasized the radicality of God's love and how we should emulate it: we should turn the other cheek, forgive seventy-seven times, give the stranger all our clothes when only our cloak was requested. Such love is incredibly generous and often quite difficult, and so it is quite often. But what often emerges from this picture is a life of hardship, a life where we turn to the other with a sense of obligation and gritted teeth, a stripped-down life as if true Christian love required us to give up everything that was fun or beautiful. Christian justice, this image suggests, is hard and radical.

I would like to suggest a different way of looking at this generosity: it is indeed radical. Yes, the extravagant love for God and of God is one that will inevitably lead to the cross, but the cross is not the final answer. If real beauty is physical, sensual, embodied, and overflowing, it will eventually die, and so much a part of beauty is our realization that it is so fleeting. We want to capture beauty, so we take touristy pictures, buy books, have plastic surgery, but in doing so we only try to put beauty in a box and refuse to let it be.

But our love of others and ourselves cannot be easily put in a box or a formula. The ability to appreciate beauty comes from a generous heart; indeed, beauty itself enlarges the heart. The sense of beauty from which I suggest we learn is akin to nature's beauty and generosity where there is always enough. To be generous with one's own beauty means to welcome others to one's self. If we can agree—as I think we can—that there is an intrinsic generosity in beauty, an openness, an invitation, then a theology of beauty that is incarnate and grows from our sense of beauty in the natural world is also a theology of generosity: to oneself and to others.

It seems to me that our contemporary images of beauty are far from generous to the self. As my friend commented about herself, everyone else looked fine, but she felt herself to be huge. Consider how our ideals of beauty are ideals of stinginess, of self-mortification, of deprivation. Consider how we talk of being good as we limit our diets, swear off chocolate or ice cream, and exercise ourselves to exhaustion. Now I am not suggesting that there is not a problem with obesity in our country and in developed nations, or that we should feel free to go on shopping expeditions whenever we feel an emptiness inside, or that we should be able to buy $600 shower curtains. What I am saying is that we have lost an ability to live generously with beauty. When we fail to acknowledge and appreciate beauty—our own, another's, nature's—we are failing to give glory to God. We are failing to love our neighbor as our self.

BEYOND UNCHANGING AND ETERNAL TRUTHS

Barbara Fiand, SNDdeN (2008)

The difficulty within Christianity, especially Catholicism, lies in our Greco-Roman heritage and its insistence on ownership of unchanging and eternal truths. When something is declared infallible (therefore, as eternal truth) to the entire Church and with an "anathema" warning for anyone who does not accept it, it becomes difficult even for serious adult believers to introduce change or to at least invite reexamination. The finalization of Christian dogma, especially in the fourth century and then throughout the centuries that followed, allowed for little variations. Even today anyone who dares to rethink the symbols and metaphors of our faith for the sake of relevance does so with trepidation.[19]

Yet the God who emerges when we give ourselves to a serious consideration of the findings of science (physics, biology, cosmology, human developmental, experimental psychology, and so on) no longer comfortably fits many of the models of our tradition. We can, of course, choose a kind of intellectual and religious dissonance—that is, study the new revelations from science but refuse to apply any of these to our spiritual quest. Much of that has happened in the past in the name of "faithfulness" to the literal teachings of Holy

Scripture. Alternatively, we can choose the less traveled road, take the risk, and allow ourselves to embrace the awe and wonder that surely will gift us when we honestly face what is offering itself to us in our day. We can then venture forth with authentic respect for, and loyalty to, our tradition, while at the same time looking for what may graciously surprise us with newness and life.

Given what we have reflected on so far, it would seem that the God of today no longer can be seen as external to the world, as above us: a God divorced from reality and working on it like the craftsman of old who rested on the seventh day when creation was finished, or even like the divine clockmaker of the Enlightenment. Creation, as we understand it today, is an ongoing, evolutionary event bursting forth from the center of the universe and continuing to expand in ever-new and extraordinary ways. God, we might say, expresses God's power there and emerges within it. In an omnicentric universe, we, and everything else with us, are at its center and, amazingly, at all times at its beginning as well. As strange and paradoxical as this may seem to the linear time-and-space categories of our mind, what it implies is that the creative energy of this universe is held in each of us.

> God operates in us and ever flows through us, energizes us, and can never be separated from us.

Concepts of God, then, as a humanlike generator of life—a father or mother; or a judge sitting on a throne above and "seeing" everything we do, punishing us by "separating" us from "himself," or rewarding us by drawing us "near"—are foreign and seem misplaced in a "sea of quantum fields," an omnicentric "space-time foam" of creativity.

More specifically, our Christian imagery of heaven as "above"—a place from which God descends, a place to which Jesus ascended after the resurrection, and a place into which Mary was assumed at her death—no longer fits into religious imagination based on the emerging world perspective. Envisioning Jesus, then, as sitting at God's right hand and coming from above in glory at the end of time to judge all of us, who will then be returned to our former embodiment, will, among other things, demand some serious "deliteralization."

These religious interpretations fit well into an understanding of a static universe with the earth as a plate and heaven as a dome covering it. They fit into a linear space/time frame with a beginning and an end of time and with space as a fixed place extended in measurable directions. An anthropomorphized version of God belonged there, and our being made "in God's image" took on physical characteristics. Ironically, this interpretation was really upside down: we made God in our image instead—with hands to hold us, feet to walk in the garden, and eyes to watch us; with a definite gender capable of impregnating a virgin; and with all the emotions of anger, vengeance, and jealousy, and the subsequent behaviors associated with human beings and projected onto the divine. Even the notions of eternity and infinity were reduced to a "no end" and "no beginning" of what we experience as linear spatial and temporal concepts.

We know today from research into the nature of light that time and space are relative. As Peter Russell, a physicist and student of consciousness, tells us: "For an observer actually traveling at the speed of light, the equations of special relativity predict that time would come to a complete standstill, and length would shrink to nothing."[20] Light, of course, travels at the speed of light. From its own perspective, therefore (if one could speak this way), it "travels no distance and takes zero time to do so."[21] This transcendence of space and time reveals something strange, indeed:

> "Whatever light is, it seems to exist in a realm where there is no before and after. There is only now,"[22] and only the here.

For us and for our commonsense appreciation of reality, this is incomprehensible, for we are used to seeing space and time as constants. For some people, as mentioned before, these constants even spill over into eternity where it is expected (dogmatically declared, in fact) that our actual bodies will find a place of rest. Others will find a place of punishment, of course, or of expiation. It is difficult for us to accept that the spatial and temporal dimensions we live in and take for granted are merely categories of our mind. We find it absurd to think of them as simply relative—as forms, in other words, of our particular mode of consciousness, not independent of it but created by it and nonapplicable in other realms of reality. But the study of light assures us that they are precisely that.

Science today agrees with the philosopher Immanuel Kant, who insisted already in the eighteenth century that we cannot see the world other than in spatial and temporal categories. "The human mind is so constituted that it is forced to construct its experience within the framework of space and time," Kant maintained. These, however, are not "fundamental dimensions of the underlying reality. They are fundamental dimensions of consciousness," that is, categories of reason.[23]

The physicist Erwin Schrödinger observes bluntly: "Every [person's] world picture is and always remains a construct of his [or her] mind, and cannot be proved to have any other existence."[24] Mystics from both East and West have, of course, generally experienced this fact, and advised us not to confuse our reality with the reality—Ultimate Reality, which, in fact, ever remains Mystery.

DIALOGUE AMID POWER INEQUITIES

Kwok Pui-Lan (2011)

As women of faiths meet and dialogue with one another, the issues of reciprocity and appropriation arise because of power differentials. Judith Plaskow, a pioneer in Jewish feminist theology, recounts the following story that provides food for thought. Some time ago she participated in a heated debate about whether a U.S. Hindologist had the right to criticize some aspects of treatment of women in Hinduism. Plaskow has studied Christian theology and has criticized Paul Tillich and Reinhold Niebuhr's doctrines of sin and grace. No one has faulted Plaskow for doing so, and in fact her work has been praised and cited by Christian feminists. Plaskow notes that the U.S. Hindologist and she receive totally different treatments because they stand in different power relationships to the tradition they were studying. Christianity is the dominant tradition in the

United States. Plaskow's critique of Christian theology would not be conceived as a threat but might even be praised for contributing to a different and more nuanced understanding of the tradition.[25] The same is not true for the U.S. white feminist who studies Hinduism. There is always the danger of Orientalism to begin with. In addition, the question of insider versus outsider perspective is a tricky one if she is not a Hindu herself. Who speaks for Hinduism has become a thorny issue, since most of the people who teach and write about Hinduism in the United States are not Hindus themselves.

Toinette M. Eugene, an African American ethicist, notes that when women of different races, classes, religions, and sexualities gather for dialogue, existing power inequities among groups must be addressed before an alternative paradigm that values mutuality can be found. She writes, "Particularity and not universality is the condition of being heard and of expressing reciprocity and mutuality in womanist/mujerista/feminist work."[26] Because of sanctioned ignorance in our educational process and learning, the diverse groups are not equal in entering dialogue, as the dominant group is not required to know the subjugated knowledges of marginalized groups. Therefore, Eugene argues that decentering of the dominant group is essential for genuine exchange to occur, such that a variety of frameworks and a variety of ways of understanding of the world can be entertained, without constantly being forced to compare to the norm of the majority or the dominant.

In antiracist work, it is important for white people to get to know the history and struggles of people of color and not depend upon the latter to educate them. Likewise, in interfaith dialogue, participants who belong to the dominant tradition need to educate themselves on other religious traditions to level the playing field. In the United States, more than seventy percent of adults identify themselves as Christian, and we hear far more references to the Bible in public discourse than to the Qur'an or the Veda. Because of the separation of church and state, students do not receive education about religious traditions in public schools. Polls have repeatedly shown that American people's religious literacy is pretty low. It is imperative to know more about other religious traditions, including the experience of both women and men, before entering into interfaith dialogue.

For Ada María Isasi-Díaz, a mujerista ethicist, respect and engagement are crucial in dialogue with others who are different from ourselves. We must respect another woman on her own terms and allow her to be herself without demanding that she act or present herself in a way that is intelligible or acceptable to us. She writes:

> We need to enter into each other's world view as much as we can and help others open up to new perspectives. Unless we are willing to do this, the self we present to people who are different from us is a "pretend self." We will hide our real selves in order to protect ourselves from others' projections of us.[27]

Only when we are prepared to engage others with honesty, Isasi-Díaz says, can we offer another person a faithful mirror to look at her tradition and allow others' work to challenge and stretch us, without reducing it to our view of it.

Critical and honest engagement in dialogue often means that we will not be the same after the encounter, after we have learned and gained helpful insights from others. The question of how to borrow and appropriate other women's perspectives and work has been a sensitive one among female scholars of religion. The issue goes beyond proper credit and acknowledgment of others' work to the motivation and intention of using others to bolster our own. Feminist ethicist Mary Hunt has cautioned that it has become customary for middle-class white feminists to cite or use women of color's work in order to show that one is politically correct or cosmopolitan. An example is the endless repetition of Alice Walker's work, as if just quoting Alice Walker will make white women look less racist. She names this intellectual crime, and says, "Such crimes are often done to give the appearance of diversity all the while maintaining the model, dynamic and framework that belong to the dominant culture into which have been shoved ideas and images that do not emerge from it."[28] The mere inclusion of a few token voices without fundamentally reconsidering the operating assumptions and epistemological framework is not true diversity. Hunt urges scholars to pay attention to the ethics of borrowing, asking such questions as why we need to borrow and how to act with reciprocity with one another.

This intellectual vigilance and honesty applies not only to interaction with women of different races and faith traditions but also to exchange within one's group. For among Jewish women, Muslim women, or Hindu women, there is a plurality of voices and differences of power. Jewish scholar Ellen M. Umansky says we need to ask, "What factors constitute sufficient similarity or commonality in deciding whose work can be appropriated?"[29] This does not mean that women scholars should feel hesitant to learn and quote from others at all, but it does mean that we acknowledge that both differences and connections exist in feminist work. Without such recognition, misuse and misappropriation of others' ideas and work will most likely occur.

Anti-Judaism and misappropriation are primary problems in Jewish-Christian dialogue and relations. Anti-Judaism has had a long history in Western history and Christian discourse. The Hebrew Scriptures have been appropriated as the Old Testament and interpreted without reference to its meaning in the Jewish tradition and rabbinic literature. The New Testament is seen as superseding the Old, since Jesus is the fulfillment of all the prophecy of the Old Testament. The new covenant brought by Jesus replaces and supersedes the old covenant between God and the Hebrew people. In parts of the New Testament, as Lawrence M. Wills has demonstrated, the Jews had been constructed as the Other and cast in negative light. This is especially so in the Gospel of John, in which the Jews are portrayed as not the true children of Abraham but the children of the devil (Jn 8:31–47).[30] Throughout Christian history, the Jews have been blamed for committing evil acts and a long trail of crimes, the most serious one being the killing of Jesus. Moreover, Judaism is seen as legalistic, governed by laws, whereas Christianity stresses faith, love, and life in the spirit. Judaism is criticized as ethnocentric and particular, while Christianity is seen as universal, inclusive, and open to all.

Judith Plaskow points out that to this long list of anti-Jewish motifs and themes, feminist interpreters of the New Testament have added "Jesus was a feminist," using Judaism as the negative foil.[31] The proponents of this view cite as evidence that no sexist saying is attributed to Jesus, while women were present among his followers. Jesus taught women, healed them, praised their faith, and used women's experience in some of his parables. But Plaskow argues that Jesus was not a feminist in the contemporary sense of the word, for "he is never portrayed as arguing for women's prerogatives, demanding changes in particular restrictive laws that affect women, or debating Pharisees on the subject of gender." In order to show that Jesus was a feminist who stood out against his background, the interpreters paint a very negative picture of the treatment of women in Judaism in Jesus's time. While Jewish men did not speak to women in public, Jesus spoke to the Samaritan woman at the well. Jesus healed the woman with a twelve-year flow of blood, while she would have been considered ritually unclean in Jewish law. Jesus praised Mary for listening to his teaching, while Martha was too busy doing the women's work. Some said that Jesus was against his Jewish culture, since women were forbidden to learn the Torah. But scholars have pointed out that Jewish views about women in Jesus's period were not monolithic, and Christian feminists have selectively chosen resources and materials to support their negative contrast. Rather than seeing Jesus's attitudes toward women as part of the spectrum of Jewish attitudes and practices, these Christian feminists claim that Jesus acted against his background and was a revolutionary.

Since anti-Semitism has led to the Holocaust and other atrocities, Christian feminists must be aware of its myriad existence in Christian culture, thought, and practices. Plaskow says that Christian feminists must recognize and problematize anti-Judaism in Christian sources and traditions as a part of their feminist analyses and discuss this issue in public. They must appreciate that Judaism is a diverse and changing tradition and not treat it as an antithesis of Christianity. In evaluating the attitude of the Jesus movement toward women, they have to take care to bring in feminist approaches to first-century Judaism. It is important to realize that rabbinic literature is not an accurate description of women's actual roles and behaviors in the first century, just as Paul's prescription about women keeping silence may not reflect women's reality at the time.[32] In fact, inscriptions have shown that Jewish women would play liturgical and leadership roles in Jewish Diaspora synagogues in Jesus's time. Plaskow also specifically addresses difficulties in Jewish-Christian dialogue. She writes, "While feminists often celebrate the ways in which women's criticism and reconstruction of religion have opened up new areas of interreligious dialogue, the reality is that much Christian feminist work takes place in isolation from the Jewish feminist agenda."[33] Christian feminists often do not know or include Jewish feminists working on similar issues, and when they invite Jewish feminists to participate in dialogue, the rules of engagement are defined on Christian terms. In order to be self-critical of Christian hegemony, an appreciation of the commonalities and differences of Jewish feminist agenda is an important step.

GOD'S ECONOMY

Christine Firer Hinze (2014)

Like modern feminism, modern Catholicism engages economic questions from a descriptive and normative perspective that emphasizes economy's inclusive, provisioning purposes and that situates markets within broader political, cultural, historical, and natural contexts. As a religious tradition that aspires to honor and embrace the fullness of reality from a God-centered perspective, Catholic Christianity roots its reflections on the mundane realities of work and markets in a perspective even deeper and wider than that of heterodox economics, one that encompasses the spiritual and the transcendent. Seeking to address credibly the economic issues of our day is, for this faith tradition, part and parcel of a calling to witness to (without ever fully controlling, much less fully comprehending) an ultimate mystery of healing Truth and Love: the one God who is Creator, Word, and Spirit, encountered by humanity in the God of Abraham, Moses, and the prophets, and most fully in the person, life, death, and resurrection of Jesus Christ. For Christians, writes Margaret Farley, "The biblical witness…claims to present a truth that will heal us, make us whole; it will free us, not enslave us to what violates our very sense of truth and justice." Its truth makes, in the words of philosopher Paul Ricoeur, a "nonviolent appeal." That which is authentically true, in this perspective, answers both "the demands of reason" and the "cries of the human heart."[34]

Christians who have encountered and set their hearts on this enlightening, beautiful, healing, and freeing truth perceive all of humanity and all of reality as created by God and, hence, valuable. Because all reality is connected to God, all is connected across space, time, and differences. The one, true God of Jesus Christ, believers affirm, abides with and can be encountered within every nook and cranny of God's creation, from the smallest, seemingly insignificant flora and fauna on earth to the cosmos's most majestic reaches. Christianity's sacramental sensibility further claims that God may be mediated and encountered in every aspect of our human species' being and doing, cultures and history.

As its central symbol of the cross (and a savior who died a tortured victim of human evil) attests, Christianity is neither sentimental nor naïve. God is present with and for humanity amid lives and histories ravaged by sin, cruelty, suffering, and life-sapping evil of all sorts. And despite Christians' confession that "our God is an on-time God," God's time frame for the provisioning, enlightenment, healing, and wholeness that suffering people and their communities seek often appears perplexingly long-term and inscrutable.

Biblical faith and human experience thus counsel sober realism concerning the limits that attempts at intra-historical transformation are likely to face. No person, policy, or institution can assure that the good will be fully served. All progress is ambiguous. But this is not the whole story. Christian realism warrants neither withdrawal from nor acquiescence to a sinful status quo. Faith and human experience also fund a theologically grounded hope that impels action for change and enables people continually to begin again even in the face of failure. "All serious and upright human conduct is hope in action," writes Pope Benedict XVI (*Spe Salvi* 35). For Christians, realism about the weight and persistence of evil, sin, and human limitation is relativized by the more comprehensive reality of the power of God's Spirit and Jesus's resurrection, continually present and working within creation and history. Using biblical vocabulary, Pope Francis writes that despite the undeniable power of sin and death, in spite of setbacks, God's kingdom of justice and wholeness continues to break into the world:

> The kingdom of God is already present in this world and is growing, here and there, and in different ways: like the small seed which grows into a great tree (cf. Mt 13:31–32), like the measure of leaven that makes the dough rise (cf. Mt 13:33) and like the good seed that grows amid the weeds (cf. Mt 13, 24–30)....The kingdom is here, it returns, it struggles to flourish anew. Christ's resurrection everywhere calls forth seeds of that new world; even if they are cut back, they grow again, for the resurrection is already secretly woven into the fabric of this history, for Jesus did not rise in vain. May we never remain on the sidelines of this march of living hope! (*Evangelii Gaudium* 278)

Over the centuries, this God-centered understanding of reality has been visualized in many ways. For our purposes, one descriptor found in Scripture and Tradition is especially apt: economy. This term, which derives from the Greek οικονομια, meaning "the management of a household," has been used in Christian theology to refer to the full compass of God's dealings with creation and humanity, as well as more particular narratives of Divine-human relations. In the eras of the New Testament and early church, the *oikos* denoted household, house, abode, dwelling place, and its inhabitants; *oikonomia*, the dynamics of sustaining and properly managing the household for the well-being of its members. Over centuries, Christians continued to use *oikonomia* to refer to God's doings with the world, including God's saving action in and through Christ; while in the wider society, economy continued to describe the management of resources and wealth within households, larger communities, and eventually, nations.

Keeping with the image of economy as a household wherein resources are produced, managed, and distributed in order to provision members' various needs, we can visualize the different sorts of economies we inhabit as an interconnected set of households within households, each with their own provisioning dynamics. We humans continuously depend upon multiple intersecting and interacting economies to supply our needs and wants, to protect our vulnerabilities, to build up and replenish our capabilities, and to provide the platforms and resources we need to survive, grow, thrive, and contribute. Metaphorically connected like Russian nesting dolls or the pieces of a puzzle, these economies are interacting environments that, quite literally, hold us in life and enable our well-being.[35]

For Christians and other believers, the most fundamental, all-encompassing household/economy is God's. Wendell Berry speaks of this as the Great Economy, his term for God's kingdom—the *oikonomia* from which nothing is excluded.[36] Embraced and held within the *oikonomia* of God, "Who was in the beginning, is now and ever shall be," is the created economy of the cosmos in all its vast variety, its ages and stages. Enfolded within this vastness, within our home galaxy and solar system, is the *oikonomia*, or global ecology, of our small, blue planet Earth, whose own interactive economies of water, air, land, and climate support the existence of biological life, from microbes and manatees to men and women.

As a species dependent on this earthly ecosphere, humanity also depends for its survival upon social interconnections within the globalized political "household" that Martin Luther King Jr. called the world house.[37] What King saw in 1964 is still the case today: this world house, this complex and highly interdependent web of polities, cultures, and nations, each with their own types of local, national, regional, and international governance, comprises essential conditions for the living and thriving of the world's peoples. Now, as in King's day, this political household is endangered and fragile. It is collapsing in part, as violence, poverty, racism, social and economic inequality, and the failures of solidarity take their toll.

Civil society, the sphere of associations that are nonmarket and nongovernment, crisscrosses and intersects larger and smaller communities. Both sustaining and dependent on political economies and civil societies are market economies, which comprise the economies of regions and nations, and local communities of cities, towns, and rural areas. Most locally, we find family and household economies, comprising individuals, kith and kin, and proximate neighbors.

Bounded but permeable matrices, these different economies provide sustaining ground, protective shelter, and vital resources that members depend upon, participate in, and, according to their capabilities, contribute to and further cultivate. What do people seek to gain by participating in these economies? Keeping with our *oikos* metaphor, we might say we seek "livelihood." But what does livelihood entail? Here again, a Christian optic provides both material and spiritual depth perception.

Writing in the 1930s about Catholic teaching's advocacy for worker justice, priest-economist Msgr. John A. Ryan summarized the elements of economic livelihood as "sufficiency, security, and status."[38] This triad of aspirations helps describe fundamental needs that people look to any economy to provide. In keeping with Catholicism's sacramental attunement, Ryan's words about the material economy can also help image what God's economy provides and enables us in turn to provide for ourselves and others.

God's Great *Oikonomia* envelops, grounds, and surpasses all the other households/economies in which we dwell. Psalm 23, likely the best-known and most beloved psalm among Christians, conjures a profound picture of this deepest, divine matrix of dependency and trust in which we live, move, and have our being. The psalmist evokes earthy images of God, the good shepherd who abundantly provides for our needs, giving us *sufficiency*; who guides and safeguards our lives, our comings and goings, giving us *security*; and dignifies us by welcoming us as members of God's own house/*oikos* for our whole lives, giving us *status*.

> The LORD is my shepherd, I shall not want.
>   He makes me lie down in green pastures;
> he leads me beside still waters;
>   he restores my soul.

He leads me in right paths
for his name's sake.

Even though I walk through the darkest valley,
I fear no evil;
for you are with me;
your rod and your staff—
they comfort me.

You prepare a table before me
in the presence of my enemies;
you anoint my head with oil;
my cup overflows.
Surely goodness and mercy shall follow me
all the days of my life,
and I shall dwell in the house [*oikos*] of the LORD
my whole life long. (NRSV)

The sufficiency, security, and status that we look to human and natural economies to provide are, as we know, never assured. As we move through our lives, observes artist Leonora Carrington, "Safety, under any circumstances, is an illusion."[39] At moments of crisis, this harsh truth becomes starkly evident and can overwhelm us. Even in ordinary circumstances, the precarity that continues to accompany us despite our best efforts can tempt us to march to a drumbeat of fear and anxiety, throwing all our energies into getting and keeping what we feel is needed to quell—or at least muffle—the terror our vulnerability evokes. Psalm 23 speaks to these fundamental fears and anxieties about our safety, our sustenance, and our well-being. Believers over centuries have sensed divine affirmation in its poetic lines: that the security and flourishing we seek is not an illusion, but a hope, a hope that is fulfilled not by our own accomplishment but in our being embraced graciously within the household and economy of the living God. Our earth and human economies reflect, at their best sacramentalize, but can never replicate or substitute for the durable security, abundant sufficiency, and graciously given status that only comes from walking with and resting in God.

Yet when it comes to engaging in social and economic life, Christians' profound theological focus on trust in God calls for believers to be neither passive nor sheep. Trust and reliance on God act as support and springboard for believers' active social engagement and contributions. Monk and spiritual writer Thomas Merton underscores each Christian's significance, giftedness, and responsibility to contribute actively to God's Great Economy through service to neighbor and world:

> Jesus…constantly reminded His hearers that the Master who had given various talents to His servants would one day return and ask for an accounting….The virtues of faith, hope, and charity, by which we are united to God, are talents given us to be developed….These gifts are given us, remember, not for ourselves alone, but for others as well. The sublime economy of divine love…demands this sharing in merits and graces….One of the most fundamental laws of life is the need to multiply itself….Good is diffusive of itself.[40]

"Every baptism," Merton continues, citing St. Paul's teaching in 1 Corinthians 12–13, "implies a distinct individual vocation, a peculiar function in the building up of the Mystical Body….Each one has something to do. We are not called merely to vegetate in the Mystical Body, but to act and to grow and to help the growth of other members."[41]

DIALOGUE AS DEEP LEARNING ABOUT GOD

Marianne Farina, CSC (2016)

Sacred conversations are interreligious dialogues and studies devoted to deep learning about God, that is, God's active presence in our own faith and action as well as in our partner's tradition. These conversations honor the integrity of religious traditions, especially by recognizing syncretistic tendencies in interpreting religious teachings and practices. The common ground becomes a shared experience of witnessing to God's transformational action in a believer's life. These interreligious encounters manifest the holiness of persons and faith communities as they strive to live their faith authentically.

Open to the movement of Spirit, sacred conversations echo Bernard Lonergan's transcendental method: "Be attentive, intelligent, reasonable, and responsible."[42] These conversations align with Lonergan's idea of conversion, which reveals self-transcending qualities of human beings[43] and the capacity for intersubjectivity facilitating the discovery of meaning, especially in the "lives and deeds of others."[44] The three dimensions of conversion are the intellectual, moral, and religious.[45] Sacred conversations reveal ways to experience personally God's call to ever-deepening faith and love, a conversion of mind and heart through *contemplative endeavors, creative freedom*, and *evolutionary consciousness* experienced as movements of God's grace in our lives.

Sacred conversations are *contemplative endeavors* that help us to become steadfast students of cultures and religions. In these engagements, we are attentive to both differences and similarities in religious teachings and practices. Keeping such "learning in the forefront," these analogues enhance our respect for one another's traditions and shape theological imaginations.[46] Sacred conversations can lead believers to an intellectual conversion by overcoming naïve realism, idealism, conceptualism, relativism, and romanticism concerning other religious beliefs and practices. Lonergan points out that "intellectual conversion is a radical clarification and, consequently, the elimination of an exceedingly stubborn and misleading myth concerning reality, objectivity, and human knowledge."[47] As sacred conversations devote energies to deep listening and feedback about knowledge shared, participants will address the misinformation about religions readily available to each religion. Thus, these engagements help each one's growth in faith. According to psychologist James Fowler, believers often remain in the conventional stage of faith development by not critically examining their beliefs.[48] Exposure to different ideas transcends the comfort zone of being "inside the institutional system" so as to grasp religious truths as "powerful forces" underlying our knowing.[49]

Sacred conversations lead to experiences of *creative freedom*. Taking responsibility for interreligious learning, the participants recognize various religious perspectives offering significant insights about God, creation, and humankind, including the concerns and aspirations of particular groups. Connections between these views and the values they express become normative. The encounters foster greater self-understanding and animate our discernment and decision-making. Thus sacred conversations facilitate our moral conversion.

These dialogues commit those engaged to pursuing true objective values that overcome conventional or personal preference. Lonergan explains the process: "As our knowledge of human reality increases, as our responses to human values are strengthened and refined, our mentors more and more leave us to ourselves so that our freedom may exercise its ever-advancing thrust toward authenticity."[50] This active solidarity was described in part one. Solidarity connects with movements in the Catholic Church such as JustFaith[51] and the Muslim community's Salam Justice and Peace Institute, which sees spiritual-moral formation as a critical component to works of justice.

Sacred conversations are holy/holistic dialogues. They gracefully embrace a freedom to be known by religious others. Those engaged learn to appreciate, even love, these connections as God loves them. We develop interreligious friendships capable of holding in esteem the mystery of God's active presence in creation. The connections lead to an *evolutionary consciousness* borne as we remain open to God's call to new depths of faith and love, greater authenticity, and a religious conversion.[52] In this modality of self-transcendence, God's love floods hearts through the Holy Spirit and becomes the ongoing dynamic of cooperation with God and others. A lack of generosity undermines this conversion. Thomas Aquinas, in his study of the virtue of charity, says that "it is more proper to charity to desire to love than to desire being loved."[53] Sacred conversations nurture this generous love necessary for religious conversion.

"Religious conversion is to a total being-in-love as the efficacious ground of all self-transcendence, whether in pursuit of truth, or the realization of human values, or in the orientation man [*sic*] adopts to the universe, its ground, and its goal."[54] Grasped by ultimate concern, converts seek ways to promote a future larger than themselves, that is, communicating in word and deed God's desire for the transformation of human hearts and relationships in a religiously complex world. Thus they can deepen respect and love for other faith traditions.

These three aspects of sacred conversations undergird a variety of dialogues, including interdisciplinary, intercultural, and interreligious. As such, these conversations become as Carl Jung described: a "spiritual adventure—the exposure of human consciousness to the undefined and the indefinable."[55] These journeys are

> [a] passing over and coming back...experimenting with the truth of life and death. In passing over to other lives, one is led to turn the truth of one's own life into poetry. This is especially clear when one comes to the point of saying to oneself, "You are what (hu)man is" and "You are what God is." Still the poetry here is not a falsification of the truth; it embodies rather deeper insight into the truth. Passing over to other lives changes one's understanding of what (hu)man is and who God is.[56]

These crossings shape a spirituality of dialogue rooted in strong faith and just action. Christians and Muslims have valuable resources for these journeys.

BECOMING SOMETHING ENTIRELY NEW

Ilia Delio, OSF (2017)

What happens when we read the New Testament in light of modern science? Today we know that nature is not static and fixed; rather, it is permeable, adaptive, creative, and transcendent. Nature can change and be changed by combining with something other than itself. The term *cyborg* (shortened for *cybernetic organism*) symbolizes the protean "nature" of nature. Cyborgs are hybrid entities of different nature whether it is animal and human or technological artifice and human. They appear where boundaries are transgressed. The cyborg disrupts persistent dualisms (such as animal and human), challenging us to search for ways to study the body as a cultural construction and a material fact of human life. The emergence of the cyborg as hybrid organism tells us something about nature that jars our prevailing understanding of nature as fixed, biological, and physical.[57] In a sense, nature has never been clearly defined. Rather, nature is an emerging process of evolving life that is now marked by a cocreation among humans and nonhumans, machines, and other partners. We cannot assume to know what is human or what is nature because what counts as human is not self-evident. Nature begins with relationships; in this respect, nature is constructed rather than given.[58]

The cyborg offers a modern symbol of the hybridization of divinity and humanity in cosmic evolution. The incarnation can be understood as cyborg since we do not have a clearly defined, exhaustive concept of humanity, let alone divinity. When the Divine Word becomes flesh (incarnation), God transcends the boundaries of separation between divinity and creation to become something new within the unfolding of space-time. God enters into bounded existence, yet these boundaries are not fixed; nature constantly transcends itself in pursuit of new, more unified life. When we confess that the Divine Word becomes flesh, we are also saying that nature has the capacity to become something new. The life of Jesus reveals the inner depth of nature to be oriented toward newness. As a hybrid creature (divinity and humanity), Jesus shows "the arbitrariness and constructed nature of what is considered the norm."[59] His life and ministry disrupt established values. Jesus as cyborg means that no one person or existent can exhaust the presence of God; God is always the more of anything that exists. Transcending boundaries and forming new relations defines the person of Jesus Christ. Anne Kull states that "the Incarnation is so contrary to common sense, it destabilizes reified categories."[60] Jesus as cyborg means that, in relation to God, the human person can become something entirely new.

Rather than emphasizing the ministry of Jesus, Teilhard suggests that we emphasize the newness of Christ. The incarnation takes place on the threshold of the future. Gerd Theissen speaks of Jesus as a biological mutation in nature. He interprets Jesus as a "protest against the principle of selection," stating that, in Jesus, "God no longer appears as a devastating power which proceeds from the pressure of selection…rather, God…makes possible life at the very point where human beings have offended against the basic conditions of reality."[61] Jesus's ethics show an alternative to selection, as Theissen writes:

> He praises eunuchs…he calls for love of enemies; he insists that outsiders are as close to us as family members; he urges his followers to be servants rather than authoritarian. All these basic demands presuppose a basic trust that the ultimate reality not only allows a much greater range of variations in human conduct, but also permits human conduct which according to the laws of biological evolution would have no chance.[62]

Jesus showed pure altruism beyond biological necessity, a complete self-dedication to others that cannot be adequately explained by principles of mutuality, cooperation, or group sympathy. Philip Hefner states, "He shows a new option for the future of cultural evolution."[63] The word *mutation* in this context means "radical changes in structures of awareness and relationship." Since a mutation is a change within the species, we can also think of Jesus as a "strange attractor," a term borrowed from chaos theory to describe a unique basin of attraction within a system that, over time, pulls the system into a new pattern of order. Jesus showed a new pattern of religious consciousness within his culture. His radical openness to God created new fields of relationships and new forms of compassionate love that broke with the juridical norms of Judaism.

The key to novelty in Jesus begins with his inner universe. Early in his ministry, the Gospels tell us, he goes out to the desert to fast and pray. He strengthens his inner world by surrendering himself completely to the Father, trusting in the immanent presence of God. This deep inner oneness with God empowers him to go out into the public and proclaim, "The kingdom of God is within you" (Lk 17:21). His life flows from inner to outer universe so that deepening his life in God gives him the courage to challenge the prevailing structures of exclusion, judgment, and condemnation.

The Gospel of John in particular emphasizes his mystical union with the Father. When Philip asks Jesus, "Where are you going? How can we know the way?" Jesus replies, "Anyone who has seen me has seen the Father" (Jn 14:9). Further on he states, "Believe me when I say that I am in the Father and the Father is in me" (Jn 14:11). We see in Jesus a deep consciousness of divine love, wholly personal and hidden, yet revealed in action. As he tells his disciples, If you do not believe my words then "at least believe on the evidence of the works themselves" (Jn 14:11). His power to do new things does not come from self-reliance but from utter reliance on God: "It is the Father, living in me, who is doing his work" (Jn 14:10). Through this inner power of love, Jesus lived on a new level of existence, free from the oppressive powers of the world and from the past. Love liberated Jesus into a new consciousness of wholeness. As Jim Marion states, "Jesus saw there was no separation between himself and any other person....He saw all human beings (and indeed the whole created universe) as part of himself."[64]

Teilhard sheds light on Jesus by saying that if God-Omega is in evolution, then we cannot find ourselves by any other means than by centering ourselves in evolution. We must give our *entire self* to God: "My ego must subsist [in Omega] through abandoning itself or the gift will fade away."[65] Evolution demands a wholehearted involvement marked by inner surrender and outer action, thus living on the edge of the unknown future: "If you wish to be my disciple you must renounce yourself, take up your cross and follow me" (Matt 16:24). Jesus calls us to self-gift by immersing ourselves in the immanent divine newness of love. His example shows us that when we live in the spirit of *agapic* love, we live in the center of freedom.

Jesus had a deep awareness of God's presence. When he was questioned by the Jews about his identity he said, "Abraham is dead, and so too are the prophets but one greater than Abraham is *here*" (Jn 8:53, author's emphasis). His consciousness of divinity impelled him to live from a new inner center of love that spontaneously flowed from his inner universe to his outer universe as he encountered others. He showed us that living in the present moment means standing on the threshold of the future, aware that every act of love is an act of freedom creating the future. In Jesus we see that life stands on the interface between the present and the future, not between the present and the past.

Appendix I

The Madeleva Manifesto

A Message of Hope and Courage

In the tradition of Sister Madeleva Wolff, CSC, we fifteen Madeleva lecturers have been invited to speak a message of hope and courage to women in the church. Reflecting the diversity of gifts bestowed on us by the Spirit, we speak from our particular experiences and vocations, yet share in a universal vision that is faithful to our catholic tradition.

- To women in ministry and theological studies, we say: reimagine what it means to be the whole body of Christ. The way things are now is not the design of God.
- To young women looking for models of prophetic leadership, we say: walk with us as we seek to follow the way of Jesus Christ, who inspires our hope and guides our concerns. The Spirit calls us to a gospel feminism that respects the human dignity of all and who inspires us to be faithful disciples, to stay in the struggle to overcome oppression of all kinds whether based on gender, sexual orientation, race, or class.
- To women who are tempted by the demons of despair and indifference, we say: reimagine what it means to

be a full human being made in the image of God, and to live and speak this truth in our daily lives.

- To women who suffer the cost of discipleship, we say: you are not alone. We remember those who have gone before us, who first held up for us the pearl of great price, the richness of Catholic thought and spirituality. We give thanks to those who continue to mentor us.
- To the young women of the church, we say: carry forward the cause of gospel feminism. We will be with you along the way, sharing what we have learned about the freedom, joy, and power of contemplative intimacy with God. We ask you to join us in a commitment to far-reaching transformation of church and society in nonviolent ways.

We deplore and hold ourselves morally bound to protest and resist, in church and society, all actions, customs, laws, and structures that treat women or men as less than fully human. We pledge ourselves to carry forth the heritage of biblical justice which mandates that all persons share in right relationship with one another, with the cosmos, and with the Creator.

We hold ourselves responsible to look for the holy in unexpected places and persons and pledge ourselves to continued energetic dialogue about issues of freedom and responsibility for women. We invite others of all traditions to join us in imagining the great shalom of God.

Feast of St. Catherine of Siena, laywoman, Doctor of the Church
April 29, 2000
Saint Mary's College, Notre Dame, Indiana

Signed by the Madeleva Lecturers in Spirituality, 1985–2001

Mary C. Boys, SNJM
Lisa Sowle Cahill
Denise Lardner Carmody
Joan Chittister, OSB
Mary Collins, OSB
Elizabeth Dreyer
Maria Harris
Diana L. Hayes
Monika K. Hellwig
M. Catherine Hilkert, OP
Elizabeth Johnson, CSJ
Dolores R. Leckey
Gail Mandell
Kathleen Norris
Jeanette Rodriguez
Sandra M. Schneiders, IHM

Appendix 2

List of Madeleva Lectures

Monika K. Hellwig, 1985
Christian Women in a Troubled World

Sandra M. Schneiders, IHM, 1986
Women and the Word: The Gender of God in the New Testament and the Spirituality of Women

Mary Collins, OSB, 1987
Women at Prayer

Maria Harris, 1988
Women and Teaching: Themes for a Spirituality of Pedagogy

Elizabeth Dreyer, 1989
Passionate Women: Two Medieval Mystics

Joan Chittister, OSB, 1990
Job's Daughters: Women and Power

Dolores Leckey, 1991
Women and Creativity

Lisa Sowle Cahill, 1992
Women and Sexuality

Elizabeth A. Johnson, CSJ, 1993
Women, Earth, and Creator Spirit

Gail Porter Mandell, 1994
Madeleva: One Woman's Life

Diana L. Hayes, 1995
Hagar's Daughters: Womanist Ways of Being in the World

Jeanette Rodriguez, 1996
Stores We Live (Cuentos Que Vivimos): *Hispanic Women's Spirituality*

Mary C. Boys, SNJM, 1997
Jewish-Christian Dialogue: One Woman's Experience

Kathleen Norris, 1998
The Quotidian Mysteries: Laundry, Liturgy, and "Women's Work"

Denise Lardner Carmody, 1999
An Ideal Church: A Meditation

Sandra M. Schneiders, IHM, 2000
With Oil in Their Lamps: Faith, Feminism, and the Future

Mary Catherine Hilkert, OP, 2001
Speaking with Authority: Catherine of Siena and the Voices of Women Today

Margaret Farley, RSM, 2002
Compassionate Respect: A Feminist Approach to Medical Ethics and Other Questions

Sidney Callahan, 2003
Women Who Hear Voices: The Challenges of Religious Experience

Mary Ann Hinsdale, IHM, 2004
Women Shaping Theology

Past Madeleva Lecturers on the 40th Anniversary of Vatican II, 2005

Susan A. Ross, 2006
For the Beauty of the Earth: Women, Sacramentality, and Justice

M. Shawn Copeland, 2007
The Subversive Power of Love: The Vision of Henriette Delille

Barbara Fiand, SNDdeN, 2008
Awe-Filled Wonder: The Interface of Science and Spirituality

Anne E. Patrick, SNJM, 2009
Women, Conscience, and the Creative Process

Wendy M. Wright, 2010
Mary and the Catholic Imagination: Le Point Vierge

Kwok Pui-Lan, 2011
Globalization, Gender, and Peacebuilding: The Future of Interfaith Dialogue

Kathleen Hughes, RSCJ, 2012
Becoming the Sign: Sacramental Living in a Post-conciliar Church

Catherine E. Clifford, 2013
Decoding Vatican II: Interpretation and Ongoing Reception

Christine Firer Hinze, 2014
Glass Ceilings and Dirt Floors: Women, Work, and the Global Economy

Voices of Young Catholic Women, A Panel Discussion, 2015

Marianne Farina, CSC, 2016
Sacred Conversations and the Evolution of Dialogue

Ilia Delio, OSF, 2017
A Hunger for Wholeness: Soul, Space, and Transcendence

Mercy Amba Oduyoye, 2018
African Women's Theologies, Spirituality, and Healing: Theological Perspectives from the Circle of Concerned African Women Theologians

Nancy Pineda-Madrid, 2019
Theologizing in an Insurgent Key: Violence, Women, Salvation

Lecture canceled due to Covid-19 pandemic, 2020

Barbara Reid, OP, 2021
At the Table of Holy Wisdom: Global Hungers and Feminist Biblical Interpretation

Lecture canceled due to lecturer health concerns, 2022

Cristina L. H. Traina, 2023
Feminism, Finitude, and Flourishing: On "Being Mortal, Like Everyone Else" (Wis 7:1)

Natalia Imperatori-Lee, 2024
Bearers of an "Idle Tale": Women's Authority in a Credibility Economy

Notes

PREFACE

1. Gail Porter Mandell, *Madeleva: One Woman's Life* (New York: Paulist Press, 1994), 4.

2. Mandell, *Madeleva*, 6–7.

3. Mandell, *Madeleva*, 7.

4. Mandell, *Madeleva*, 7.

5. Mandell, *Madeleva*, 10–11.

6. Mandell, *Madeleva*, 33.

7. Mandell, *Madeleva*, 31–37.

8. Mandell, *Madeleva*, 3–4.

9. Mandell, *Madeleva*, 41.

10. Mandell, *Madeleva*, 41.

11. Mandell, *Madeleva*, 41.

12. Keith J. Egan, "The Center for Spirituality, Saint Mary's College, Notre Dame, Indiana: A Proposal Submitted to the Board of Regents," unpublished document, Center for the Study of Spirituality Archives (March 23, 1984), 2.

13. Email correspondence with Keith J. Egan on February 28, 2024.

14. Phone interview with Keith J. Egan on February 29, 2024.

15. The request for and confirmation of the financial gift is found in the following letters: John M. Duggan, "Letter to Sister Olivia Marie Hutcheson, CSC," unpublished letter, Center for the Study of Spirituality Archives (May 18, 1984); Sister Olivia Marie, CSC, "Letter to Dr. John M. Duggan, President of Saint Mary's College," unpublished

letter, Center for the Study of Spirituality Archives (June 4, 1984); and Sister Olivia Marie, CSC, "Letter to Dr. John M. Duggan, President of Saint Mary's College," unpublished letter, Center for the Study of Spirituality Archives (June 21, 1984).

16. Egan, "The Center for Spirituality, 5.

17. Email correspondence with Keith J. Egan on February 28, 2024.

18. Phone interview with Keith J. Egan on February 29, 2024.

19. Phone interview with Keith J. Egan on February 29, 2024.

20. Patricia Sullivan, "GU Theologian, Catholic Activist Monika Hellwig Dies," *The Washington Post* (October 6, 2005).

21. Monika K. Hellwig, *Christian Women in a Troubled World* (New York: Paulist Press, 1985), 1.

22. Nancy Pineda-Madrid, *Theologizing in an Insurgent Key: Violence, Women, Salvation* (New York: Paulist Press, 2022).

Chapter I: PRAYER AND SPIRITUALITY

1. Adrienne Rich, *Of Woman Born* (New York: W. W. Norton, 1976), 11.

2. Rich, *Of Woman Born*, 11. Emphasis in the original.

3. See Bernard Lonergan, *Insight* (San Francisco: Harper & Row, 1957), 187–94, for a discussion of avoidance of insight through the repression of images.

4. Rosemary Cingari, "Lost, Hidden or Broken Images" (unpublished manuscript).

5. Carol Christ, "Spiritual Quest and Women's Experience," in *Womanspirit Rising*, ed. Carol P. Christ and Judith Plaskow (New York: Harper and Row, 1979), 230.

6. Margaret Atwood, *Surfacing* (New York: Simon and Schuster, 1972), 222–23.

7. Adrienne Rich, "Taking Women Students Seriously," *The Radical Teacher* 11 (March 1979): 42.

8. Rich, "Taking Women Students Seriously," 42.

9. Ntozake Shange, *for colored girls who have considered suicide/ when the rainbow is enuf* (New York: Macmillan, 1976), 66.

10. See Irving Greenberg, *The Jewish Way: Living the Holidays*, repr. ed. (New York: Touchstone, 1993).

11. Abraham Joshua Heschel, *The Sabbath: Its Meaning for Modern Man* (New York: Farrar, Straus and Giroux, 1951), 13. I have changed the text to make his language inclusive of women.

12. Luke Timothy Johnson, *Faith's Freedom* (Minneapolis: Fortress, 1990), 65.

13. Dorothy C. Bass, "Keeping Sabbath," in *Practicing Our Faith: A Way of Life for a Searching People*, ed. Dorothy Bass (San Francisco: Jossey-Bass, 1997), 86.

14. See John C. Merkle, "The Challenge of Jewish Spirituality to Christian Faith," in *Proceedings of the Center for Jewish-Christian Learning*, ed. Arthur E. Zannoni, 6 (1991): 32–37.

15. Chaim Stern, ed., *Gates of Prayer for Weekdays* (New York: Central Conference of American Rabbis, 1975), 36.

16. In Marge Piercy, *Available Light* (New York: Alfred Knopf), 123. For details of this prayer in Jewish liturgy, see Macy Nulman, *The Encyclopedia of Jewish Prayer* (Northvale, NJ: Jason Aronson, 1993), 255–56.

17. See Carol Ochs, *Women and Spirituality* (Notre Dame, IN: University of Notre Dame Press, 1983) and *Song of the Self* (Philadelphia: Trinity Press International, 1994); Daniel Gordis, *God Was Not in the Fire: The Search for a Spiritual Judaism* (New York: Scribners, 1995); and David J. Wolpe, *In Speech and in Silence* (New York: Henry Holt, 1992).

18. Everett Fox, *The Five Books of Moses: A New Translation with Introductions, Commentary and Notes* (New York: Schocken Books, 1995), xxix and 273.

19. See Maurice Friedman, *Martin Buber: The Life of Dialogue*, 3rd ed. (Chicago: University of Chicago Press, 1976). I am indebted to Sandra Lubarsky for this reference.

20. I think not only of the corpus of the writings of Elie Wiesel, but also of David R. Blumenthal, *Facing the Abusing God: A Theology of Protest* (Louisville, KY: Westminster/John Knox, 1993).

21. See Anson Laytner, *Arguing with God: A Jewish Tradition* (Northvale, NJ: Jason Aronson, 1990).

Chapter 2: THE CHURCH

1. See Congregation for the Clergy, "The Priest: Teacher of the Word, Minister of the Sacraments, and Leader of the Community," *Origins* 29, no. 13 (September 9, 1999): 202, and Eight Vatican Offices, "Instruction: On Certain Questions Regarding the Collaboration of the Nonordained Faithful in the Sacred Ministry of Priests," *Origins* 27/24 (November 27, 1997): *passim*.

2. Sister Theresa Kane, RSM, "Welcome to Pope John Paul II," October 7, 1979, from the Archives of the Leadership Conference of Women Religious, CLCW 54/47, University of Notre Dame Archives, Notre Dame, IN.

3. See the Archives of the Leadership Conference of Women Religious, Correspondence 1979–80, CLCW 36/7, and Consortium Perfectae Caritatis, Administrative Meeting, November 14, 1979, CMAS 3/30, University of Notre Dame Archives, Notre Dame, IN.

4. J. M. R. Tillard, "Sensus Fidelium," *One in Christ* 11 (1975): 24.

5. Elisabeth Schüssler Fiorenza, *Discipleship of Equals: A Critical Feminist Ekklesia-logy of Liberation* (New York: Crossroad, 1993), 3.

6. Rosemary Radford Ruether, "Autobiographical Roots of Dialogue," in Rita M. Gross and Rosemary Radford Ruether, *Religious Feminism and the Future of the Planet* (New York: Continuum, 2001), 56–58.

7. Joan Chittister, *In Search of Belief* (Ligouri, MO: Ligouri Publications, 1999), 171–72.

8. Mary Jo Weaver, *Springs of Water in a Dry Land: Spiritual Survival for Catholic Women Today* (Boston: Beacon Press, 1993), xii.

9. Mary Jo Weaver, "Cancer in the Body of Christ," in *Women's Spirituality: Resources for Christian Development*, 2nd ed., ed. Joann Wolski Conn (New York: Paulist Press, 1996), 68–82.

10. Weaver, "Cancer in the Body of Christ," 69.

11. Weaver, "Cancer in the Body of Christ," 75.

12. Steven Levine, *Healing into Life and Death* (New York: Doubleday, 1982), 30. Cited in Weaver, "Cancer in the Body of Christ," 73.

13. Weaver, "Cancer in the Body of Christ," 74.

14. Rowan Williams, *The Wound of Knowledge: Christian Spirituality from the New Testament to St. John of the Cross* (Boston: Cowley Publications, 1990), 12. Cited in Weaver, "Cancer in the Body of Christ," 76.

15. Weaver, "Cancer in the Body of Christ," 77.

16. Weaver, "Cancer in the Body of Christ," 77.

17. Weaver, "Cancer in the Body of Christ," 78.

18. Rite of Christian Initiation of Adults, 245, 247.

19. Romano Guardini, *Sacred Signs,* trans. Grace Branham (St. Louis, MO: Pio Decimo Press, 1956), 13–14.

20. Guardini, *Sacred Signs*, 10.

21. The Catechesis of the Good Shepherd program (CGS) is a perfect example of Guardini's conviction that very young children can receive religious formation through all the symbolic languages of the liturgy and that the nascent religious sensibilities of the very young can most easily be fanned into flame. CGS takes a child's religious experience seriously and uses biblical and liturgical components to nurture that experience of God.

22. This observation was made by a Protestant observer, Douglas Horton, *Vatican Diary: A Protestant Observer to the Fourth Session of Vatican Council II*, vol. 3 (Philadelphia: United Church Press, 1964–67), 165.

23. Of particular importance were the interventions of Cardinal Suenens and Melkite Archbishop George Hakim on October 23 and 24, 1964, respectively.

24. Rosemary Goldie, "Lay Participation in the Work of Vatican II," *Miscellenia Lateranense "Lateranum"* (1974–75).

25. Carmel McEnroy, *Guests in Their Own House: The Women at Vatican II* (New York: Crossroad, 1996), 139–44.

26. McEnroy, *Guests in Their Own House*, 146–54.

27. An English translation of his speech, delivered October 23, 1964, appears in: "Patrick Keegan," *Council Daybook: Vatican II*, vol. 2, Floyd Anderson, ed. (Washington, DC: National Catholic Welfare Conference, 1965), 131–32.

28. Cited in McEnroy, *Guests in Their Own House*, 145.

29. Cited in Mary Luke Tobin, "Women in the Church Since Vatican II," *America*, November 1, 1986, http://americamagazine.org/issue/100/women-church-vatican-ii.

30. Cited in McEnroy, *Guests in Their Own House*, 156.

31. Gertrud Heinzelmann, *Wir schweigen nicht länger! Frauen äussern sich zum II Vatikanischen Konzil* (Zürich: Interfeminas-Verlag, 1965).

32. During his pontificate, the Congregation for the Doctrine of the Faith issued a declaration on the question of women's ordination, enlisting the unfortunate argument that only males are suited to "act in the place of Christ." "Declaration *Inter Insignores*, on the Admission of Women to the Ordained Priesthood [1976]," http://www.vatican.va/roman_curia/congregations/cfaith/documents/rc_con_cfaith_doc_19761015_inter-insigniores_en.html.

33. John Paul II, "Apostolic Letter *Ordinatio Sacerdotalis, On Reserving the Ordained Priesthood to Men Alone* [1994]," http://www.vatican.va/holy_father/john_paul_ii/apost_letters/documents/hf_jp-ii_apl_22051994_ordinatio-sacerdotalis_en.html.

Chapter 3: HOLY WOMEN

1. Mary Owens, OP, "Women in the Convent," in *American Catholic Women: A Historical Exploration*, ed. Karen Kennelly, CSJ (New York: Macmillan, 1989), 17.

2. See the 1989 Madeleva Lecture published as: Elizabeth Dryer, *Passionate Women: Two Medieval Mystics* (New York/Mahwah: Paulist Press, 1989).

3. Octavio Paz, *Sor Juana*, trans. Margaret Sayers Peden (Cambridge, MA: Harvard University Press, 1988).

4. Paz, *Sor Juana*, 109.

5. For insights into the relationship between solitude and creativity, see May Sarton, *Journal of a Solitude* (New York: W. W. Norton, 1973).

6. Paz, *Sor Juana*, 136.

7. May Sarton, *Writings on Writing* (Orono, ME: Puckerbrush Press, 1980), 40.

8. Paz, *Sor Juana*, 102.
9. Paz, *Sor Juana*, 304.
10. Paz, *Sor Juana*, 304.
11. Paz, *Sor Juana*, 424.
12. Charles Davis, *The Body as Spirit: The Nature of Religious Feeling* (New York: Seabury Press, 1976), 151.
13. Jeanette Rodríguez, *Our Lady of Guadalupe: Faith and Empowerment among Mexican-American Women* (Austin: University of Texas Press, 1994).
14. Wendy Doniger O'Flaherty, *Other People's Myths* (New York: Macmillan, 1988), 27.
15. Eric R. Wolf, "The Virgin of Guadalupe: A Mexican National Symbol," *Journal of American Folklore* 71 (1958): 34–49.
16. Johannes Baptist Metz, *Faith in History and Society: Toward a Practical, Fundamental Theology*, trans. N. D. Smith (New York: Crossroad, 1980), 184.
17. Metz, *Faith in History and Society*, 184.
18. Metz, *Faith in History and Society*, 184.
19. Metz, *Faith in History and Society*, 184.
20. Metz, *Faith in History and Society*, 200.
21. Bernard Lonergan, *Method in Theology* (New York: Herder & Herder, 1972), 240.
22. Rosemary Haughton, *The Passionate God* (New York: Paulist Press, 1981).
23. Lonergan, *Method in Theology*, 109.
24. Metz, *Faith in History and Society*, 106, 111.
25. John of the Cross, *The Collected Works of St. John of the Cross*, rev. ed., trans. Kiernan Kavanaugh and Otilio Rodriguez (Washington, DC: ICS Publications, 1991), "The Ascent of Mount Carmel," Book Two, chap. 17, no. 5, 207.
26. Constance FitzGerald, "Transformation in Wisdom: The Subjective Character and Educative Power of Sophia in Contemplation," in *Carmel and Contemplation: Transforming Human Consciousness*, ed. Kevin Culligan and Regis Jordan (Washington, DC: ICS Publications, 2000), 290–91.

27. Kathleen Margaret Williams, "Lonergan and the Transforming Immanence of The Transcendent: Towards a Theology of Grace as the Dynamic State of Being-in-Love with God" (DTheol diss., Melbourne College of Divinity, 1998), 154.

28. William Johnston, *Mystical Theology: The Science of Love* (London: Harper Collins, 1995), 255.

29. Sandra M. Schneiders in her *Religious Life in a New Millennium*, vol. 2, *Selling All: Commitment, Consecrated Celibacy, and Community in Catholic Religious Life* (New York/Mahwah, NJ: Paulist Press, 2001) distinguishes virginity, chastity, and consecrated celibacy. Here I use the term *chastity*, as it seems more appropriate to nineteenth-century consecrated religious life.

30. See Josephine Massingberd Ford, *A Trilogy on Wisdom and Celibacy* (Notre Dame, IN: University of Notre Dame Press, 1967); Peter Brown, *The Body and Society, Men, Women, and Sexual Renunciation in Early Christianity* (New York: Columbia University Press, 1988).

31. Schneiders, *Selling All*, 182.

32. Schneiders, *Selling All*, 183.

33. Facsimile of "The Rules and Regulations for the Congregation of the Sisters of the Presentation of the Blessed Virgin Mary under the Invocation of Mary the Virgin of the Holy Presentation. Founded in New Orleans the 21st November 1836." The French original is in the Archives of the Sisters of the Holy Family, New Orleans, Louisiana.

34. Virginia Meacham Gould and Charles E. Nolan, "Introduction," in Sister Mary Bernard Deggs, *No Cross, No Crown: Black Nuns in Nineteenth-Century New Orleans*, ed. Virginia Meacham Gould and Charles E. Nolan (Bloomington: Indiana University Press, 2001), xxxi; Cyprian Davis, *Henriette Delille: Servant of Slaves, Witness to the Poor* (New Orleans: Archdiocese of New Orleans/Sisters of the Holy Family, 2004), 21.

35. Lonergan, *Method in Theology*, 327.

36. Davis, *Henriette Delille*, 78.

37. Sister Mary Bernard Deggs, *No Cross, No Crown: Black Nuns in Nineteenth-Century New Orleans*, ed. Virginia Meacham Gould and Charles E. Nolan (Bloomington: Indiana University Press, 2001), 9.

38. Deggs, *No Cross, No Crown*, 9–10.

39. Deggs, *No Cross, No Crown*, 12.

40. Deggs, *No Cross, No Crown*, 46.

41. William R. Jones, *Is God a White Racist? A Preamble to Black Theology* (Garden City, NY: Anchor, 1973), 21–22.

42. Constance FitzGerald, "Impasse and Dark Night," in Joann Wolski Conn, ed., *Women's Spirituality: Resources for Christian Development* (Mahwah, NJ: Paulist Press, 1986), 299.

43. Bernard Lonergan, *Insight: A Study of Human Understanding* (New York: Philosophical Library, 1957), 699, 721–23.

44. Deggs, *No Cross, No Crown*, 46.

45. I discuss this topic more fully in Anne E. Patrick, *Liberating Conscience: Feminist Explorations in Catholic Moral Theology* (New York: Continuum, 1997), 185–88.

46. See Ellen Whelan, OSF, *The Sisters' Story: Saint Mary's Hospital—Mayo Clinic 1839–1939* (Rochester, MN: Mayo Foundation for Medical Education and Research, 2002), 44. Whelan's chronicle adds that several sisters shared the reluctance initially voiced by Dr. Mayo. The July 1886 record of the sisters' executive council counted twenty-seven votes in favor and four against building the hospital (46).

47. *The Education of Sister Lucy* (Notre Dame, IN: Saint Mary's College, 1949). Madeleva's name is not given as editor, but she had invited the papers and written the opening and concluding essays: "The Education of Our Young Religious Teachers," in which the hypothetical Sister Lucy's educational needs are described (5–10), and "The Preparation of Teachers of Religion in College" (35–39).

48. Gail Porter Mandell, *Madeleva: A Biography* (Albany: State University of New York Press, 1997), 189. See also Karen Kennelly's recent history of the movement, *The Religious Formation Conference 1954–2004* (Silver Spring, MD: Religious Formation Conference, 2009).

49. Sandra M. Schneiders, in addition to being a prolific writer on biblical studies, spirituality, and religious life, has served as president of the Society for the Study of Christian Spirituality and also the Catholic Biblical Association of America. Her Madeleva Lectures are *Women and the Word* (Mahwah, NJ: Paulist Press, 1986) and *With Oil in Their Lamps: Faith, Feminism, and the Future* (Mahwah, NJ: Paulist Press, 2000). Mary Ann Hinsdale was elected vice president of

the Catholic Theological Society of America (CTSA) in 2008, with automatic succession to the presidency in 2010–2011. Her Madeleva Lecture, *Women Shaping Theology* (Mahwah, NJ: Paulist Press, 2006), mentions (84) that the first two women members of the CTSA, who joined in 1965, were graduates of the doctoral program at Saint Mary's College: Cathleen M. Going (1956) and Elizabeth Farians (1958).

50. See Margaret R. Brennan, IHM, *What Was There for Me Once: A Memoir* (Toronto: Novalis, 2009), and Mary Ellen Sheehan, Mary Heather MacKinnon, and Moni McIntyre, eds., *Light Burdens, Heavy Blessings: Challenges of Church and Culture in the Post Vatican II Era: Essays in Honor of Margaret R. Brennan* (Quincy, IL: Franciscan Press, 2000).

51. Mandell, *Madeleva*, 185.

52. Daly's studies in Europe took place during the Second Vatican Council, and she was inspired by the energy for reform to publish *The Church and the Second Sex* (New York: Harper & Row, 1968). This hopeful, scholarly volume reviewed the history of sexism in the Catholic Church and offered some "modest proposals" for reform. It did not, however, win Daly tenure at Boston College, though that decision was eventually reversed in Daly's favor after student protesters took up her cause. By that time, however, Daly's patience as a Catholic reformer had been exhausted, and, like Martin Luther before her, she grew much more radical. Thus in October 1971, during a famous sermon in Harvard Memorial Chapel, she boldly declared Christianity and all patriarchal religions to be morally bankrupt and urged her followers, women and men, to walk out of the chapel in a symbolic exodus from patriarchy. See Mary Daly, "The Women's Movement: An Exodus Community," *Religious Education* 67 (September October 1972). 327–33; most of this sermon is reprinted in Elizabeth A. Clark and Herbert Richardson, eds., *Women and Religion: The Original Sourcebook of Women in Christian Thought*, rev. ed. (HarperSanFrancisco, 1996), 311–18. Two years later Daly published *Beyond God the Father: Toward a Philosophy of Women's Liberation* (Boston: Beacon, 1973), a theoretical rejection of Christian theology, whose arguments have since been countered in major works by feminist theologians, including Rosemary Radford Ruether, *Sexism and God Talk: Toward a Feminist Theology* (Boston: Beacon, 1983); Anne E. Carr, *Transforming*

Grace: Christian Tradition and Women's Experience (New York: Harper & Row, 1988); and Elizabeth A. Johnson, *She Who Is: The Mystery of God in Feminist Theological Discourse* (New York: Continuum, 1992). Daly has provided autobiographical information in the "New Feminist Postchristian Introduction" to the 1975 edition of *The Church and the Second Sex* (New York: Harper & Row), and also in *Outercourse: The Be-Dazzling Voyage* (HarperSanFrancisco, 1992).

53. See, for example, the special issue of *Creativity Research Journal* 20, no. 2 (2008) on "Malevolent Creativity."

54. I discuss this case more fully in Patrick, *Liberating Conscience*, 45–48. Earlier, theologian Margaret A. Farley, a Sister of Mercy, offered an insightful analysis in "Power and Powerlessness: A Case in Point," *CTSA Proceedings* 37 (1982): 116–19, noting that the decision should continue to be reexamined and that the choice of the Sisters of Mercy to remain silent at the time was made in the hope "that theirs and other voices may ultimately prevail." She also acknowledged that there was a danger in the "unfinished story" she had told, namely, "that the silence will grow, and that the power in the Church will be more and more isolated, especially from the experience of women" (119).

55. Merton was undoubtedly familiar with the traditional Marian resonance of the term as was Massignon, but it seems to have struck him anew in the context of the correspondence, which dealt with political and social issues as well as with Sufism.

56. Dorothy C. Buck translates the phrase this way. See her "The Theme of *Le Point Vierge* in the Writings of Louis Massignon." Available http://www.dcbuck.com/Talks/Massignon.html.

57. The most thorough article on Merton and Massignon and *le point vierge* is by Sidney H. Griffith, "Thomas Merton, Louis Massignon and the Challenge of Islam," *The Merton Annual* 3 (1990): 151–73. I am indebted to Christian Krokus for his helpful explanation of *le point vierge* in the writings of Massignon.

58. Thomas Merton, *Witness to Freedom: The Letters of Thomas Merton in Times of Crisis*, ed. William H. Shannon (New York: Farrar Straus Giroux, 1989), 278.

59. Thomas Merton, *Conjectures of a Guilty Bystander* (New York: Doubleday, 1968), 151.

60. I hope I do this in concert with a number of other feminist scholars who could well be said to be engaged in writing Third Wave Mariology. Sarah Jane Boss in Wales and Tina Beattie in England as well as Aurelie Hagstrom and Charlene Spretnak here in the United States—each approaches the topic of Mary from divergent perspectives, but they all take up traditional titles and attributes applied to the Virgin and turn them in new directions.

61. William F. Lynch, SJ, "Theology and the Imagination," *Thought* 29 (Spring 1954): 76.

62. Matovina describes the symbol of Guadalupe at San Fernando Mission as encompassing patriotism, political protest, divine retribution and covenant renewal, ethnic solidarity and reinforcement of social hierarchy, a model of feminine virginity and domesticity and an inspiration for women to be active in the public arena and demand equality, a plea for miraculous intervention, and an inducement for greater participation in the Church's sacramental life. She "also provided a ritual arena for Mexicans and Mexican-Americans to forge and celebrate an alternative world, one in which powerful realities like exile and racism could be defined and re-imagined. A brown skinned 'exile' herself Guadalupe was a treasured companion whose faithful encountered her most intensely in the midst of the displacement discrimination, degradation, and all the difficulties they endured." See Timothy Matovina, *Guadalupe and Her Faithful: Latino Catholics in San Antonio from Colonial Origins to the Present* (Baltimore: Johns Hopkins University Press, 2005).

63. Thomas Merton, *Contemplative Prayer* (New York: Image Books, 1996), 67.

64. Of course, Mary has long held the title *tota pulchra*, the all beautiful. On this see the excellent article by Johann G. Roten, SM, "Mary and the Way of Beauty," *Marian Studies* 49 (1998): 109–27. Even in this article, however, and certainly in magisterial statements, I find that the language of beauty—she is "the all beautiful creature, the mirror without stain, the supreme ideal of perfection"—tends to be rather static and locked into a European aesthetic. It feels somehow overly concerned with docility, purity, and correctness. The experience of the rich cultural diversity in Los Angeles and the living presence of Mary in those communities open up the experience of beauty.

The imaginative language of beauty, visual and linguistic, here seems to me to "sing." It feels expansive, passionate, prophetic, and complicated, and thus true to experience.

Chapter 4: GENDER AND SEXUALITY

1. E.g., Gordon D. Kaufman, *The Theological Imagination: Constructing the Concept of God* (Philadelphia: Westminster, 1981); Ray L. Hart, *Unfinished Man and the Imagination: Toward an Ontology and Rhetoric of Revelation* (New York: Herder and Herder, 1968).

2. E.g., Patrick W. Collins, *More Than Meets the Eye: Ritual and Parish Liturgy* (New York: Paulist Press, 1983).

3. E.g., John Shea, *Stories of God: An Unauthorized Biography* (Chicago: Thomas More, 1978) and *An Experience Named Spirit* (Chicago: Thomas More, 1983).

4. Elisabeth Schüssler Fiorenza, *In Memory of Her: A Feminist Theological Reconstruction of Christian Origins* (New York: Crossroad, 1983), 160–204.

5. See Irving Singer, *The Nature of Love*, vol. 2 (Cambridge, MA: MIT Press, 2009), 32.

6. Rosemary Haughton, *The Passionate God* (New York: Paulist Press, 1981); and *On Trying to Be Human* (Springfield, IL: Templegate, 1966).

7. Haughton, *On Trying to Be Human*, 93.

8. Haughton, *On Trying to Be Human*, 106.

9. Haughton, *On Trying to Be Human*, 9.

10. Haughton, *On Trying to Be Human*, 18.

11. Haughton, *On Trying to Be Human*, 21.

12. Haughton, *On Trying to Be Human*, 27.

13. Haughton, *On Trying to Be Human*, 26.

14. Haughton, *On Trying to Be Human*, 7.

15. Haughton, *On Trying to Be Human*, 6.

16. Haughton, *On Trying to Be Human*, 6.

17. Milton Viederman lists as enemies of passion: total understanding of the other, familiarity, certainty, predictability, absolute trust in the other, the disarming of jealousy and legitimization of the relationship. Viederman, "The Nature of Passionate Love," in *Passionate*

Attachments: Thinking about Love, ed. Willard Gaylin and Ethel Person (New York: Free Press, 1988), 6. This list suggests a legitimate but limited understanding of passion. In fact, elements of this kind of passion are inimical to mystical experience inasmuch as the passion of mysticism is predicated on trust in God and a definite kind of legitimacy. However, some of the "enemies" listed by Viederman are reflected in accounts of mystical passion, such as God's jealousy, lack of total understanding of God by the mystic, a certain lack of familiarity since the partner in the relationship is ultimate Mystery, and so forth.

18. *The Book of Job*, trans. Stephen Mitchell (San Francisco: North Point Press, 1987).

19. *The Book of Job*, 3.

20. *The Book of Job*, 6.

21. *The Book of Job*, 35.

22. *The Book of Job*, 41.

23. *The Book of Job*, 44.

24. *The Book of Job*, 45.

25. *The Book of Job*, 59.

26. *The Book of Job*, 58.

27. *The Book of Job*, 64.

28. *The Book of Job*, 71.

29. *The Book of Job*, 91.

30. *The Book of Job*, 91.

31. Evelyn Eaton Whitehead and James D. Whitehead, *A Sense of Sexuality: Christian Love and Intimacy* (New York: Doubleday, 1988), 22, 23.

32. Alice Walker, *In Search of Our Mothers' Gardens: Womanist Prose* (New York: Harcourt Brace Jovanovich, 1983), 231.

33. Walker, *In Search of Our Mothers' Gardens*, 231.

34. Walker, *In Search of Our Mothers' Gardens*, 76.

35. Walker, *In Search of Our Mothers' Gardens*, 74.

36. Walker, *In Search of Our Mothers' Gardens*, 234.

37. Bernice Johnson Reagon, "Africa Diaspora Women: The Making of Cultural Workers," in *Women in Africa and the African Diaspora*, ed. Rosalyn Terborg-Penn, Sharon Harley, and Andrea Benton Rushing (Washington, DC: Howard University Press, 1987), 167–80; 169.

38. Johnson Reagon, "Africa Diaspora Women: The Making of Cultural Workers," 177.

39. Gay Wilentz, *Binding Cultures: Black Women Writers in Africa and the Diaspora* (Bloomington: Indiana University Press, 1992), xx.

40. Jacquelyn Grant, "Black Women and the Church," in *But Some of Us Are Brave: Black Women's Studies*, ed. Akasha (Gloria T.) Hull, Patricia Bell-Scott, and Barbara Smith (New York: Feminist Press, 1982), 144.

41. Margaret Busby, ed., *Daughters of Africa* (New York: Pantheon Books, 1992), xxxvii.

42. Busby, *Daughters of Africa*, xxxxi.

43. Wilentz, *Binding Cultures*, xxviii–xxix.

44. Grant, "Black Women and the Church," 141–52; 147.

45. Walker, *In Search of Our Mothers' Gardens*, xi.

46. Pope John Paul II, *Mulieris Dignitatem* (On the Dignity of Women), August 15, 1988, https://www.vatican.va/content/john-paul-ii/en/apost_letters/1988/documents/hf_jp-ii_apl_19880815_mulieris-dignitatem.html.

47. Sidney Callahan, "Self and Other in Feminist Thought," in *Duties to Others*, ed. Courtney S. Campbell and B. Andrew Lustig (Boston: Kluwer Academic Publishers, 1994), 55–69.

48. Alice H. Eagly and Wendy Wood, "The Origins of Sex Differences in Human Behavior Evolved Dispositions Versus Social Roles," *American Psychologist* 54, no. 6 (June 1999): 408–23.

49. Rodney Stark, *The Rise of Christianity: A Sociologist Reconsiders History* (Princeton, NJ: Princeton University Press, 1996).

50. Caroline Walker Bynum, *Jesus as Mother: Studies in the Spirituality of the High Middle Ages* (Berkeley: University of California Press, 1982).

51. Ron Hansen, *A Stay Against Confusion: Essays on Faith and Fiction* (New York: HarperCollins, 2001), 180.

52. Denise M. Ackermann, "From Mere Existence to Tenacious Endurance Stigma: HIV/AIDS and Feminist Theory and Praxis," in *African Women, Religion, and Health: Essays in Honor of Mercy Amba Ewudziwa Oduyoye*, ed. Isabel Apawo Phiri and Sarojini Nadar (Eugene, OR: Wipf & Stock, 2012), 235.

53. Fulata Lusungu Moyo, "Navigating Experiences of Healing: A Narrative Theology of Eschatological Hope as Healing," in *African Women, Religion, and Health: Essays in Honor of Mercy Amba Ewudziwa Oduyoye*, ed. Isabel Apawo Phiri and Sarojini Nadar (Eugene, OR: Wipf & Stock, 2012), 244.

54. Ackermann, "From Mere Existence to Tenacious Stigma," 226.

55. Hajia Katumi Mahama, "Empowering Muslim Women for the Third Millennium," in *Women in Religion and Culture: Essays in Honour of Constance Buchanan*, ed. Mercy Amba Oduyoye (Ibadan, Nigeria: Sefer, 2007), 156.

56. Fulata Lusungu Moyo, "Navigating Experiences of Healing," in *African Women, Religion, and Health: Essays in Honor of Mercy Amba Ewudziwa Oduyoye*, ed. Isabel Apawo Phiri and Sarojini Nadar (Eugene, OR: Wipf & Stock, 2012), 244–53.

57. Moyo, "Navigating Experiences of Healing," 244.

58. Moyo, "Navigating Experiences of Healing," 252.

59. Moyo, "Navigating Experiences of Healing," 253.

60. Roger Haight, *Jesus Symbol of God* (Maryknoll, NY: Orbis, 1999), 335.

61. The phrase *kingdom of God* is not gender inclusive and, along with many feminist theologians, I most often use the word *reign* instead. However, *kingdom of God* denotes a geographic region in which God's will is fully realized. This is the connotation I wish to invoke in this passage; hence my use of the phrase.

62. Haight, *Jesus Symbol of God*, 340.

63. Jon Sobrino, *Jesus the Liberator: A Historical-Theological View* (Maryknoll, NY: Orbis, 1993), 160.

64. Sobrino, *Jesus the Liberator*, 93, 53, 85.

65. Josiah Royce, *Studies of Good and Evil: A Series of Essays upon Problems of Philosophy and of Life* (New York: D. Appleton and Company, 1898), 23.

66. Josiah Royce, *The Sources of Religious Insight* (New York: Charles Scribner's Sons, 1912), 252–55.

67. Haight, *Jesus Symbol of God*, 344–45.

68. Augustine, *Confessions*, X.6; Aquinas, *Summa Theologiae*, I, q.47, a.1.

69. Elizabeth A. Johnson, CSJ, *Creation: Is God's Charity Broad Enough for Bears?* (Los Angeles: Marymount Institute Press, 2014), 9–11.

70. Josiah Royce, *The Problem of Christianity* (Chicago: University of Chicago Press, 1918), 223, 337–42, 362, 374–84.

71. Haight, *Jesus Symbol of God*, 383.

72. Royce, *Sources of Religious Insight*, 266.

73. Royce, *Sources of Religious Insight*, 266–67.

74. Haight, *Jesus Symbol of God*, 387.

75. Haight, *Jesus Symbol of God*, 383, 355–56.

76. Royce, *Studies of Good and Evil*, 23.

77. Haight, *Jesus Symbol of God*, 356.

78. Haight, *Jesus Symbol of God*, 374–75.

Chapter 5: CULTURE AND DIALOGUE

1. In addition to Irene Diamond and Gloria Orenstein, *Reweaving the World* (Oakland, CA: Sierra Club Books, 1990), which has an extended bibliography, see Judith Plante, ed., *Healing the Wounds: The Promise of Ecofeminism* (Philadelphia: Fortress, 1984); and Lois Daly, "Ecofeminism, Reverence for Life, and Feminist Theological Ethics," in *Liberating Life: Contemporary Approaches to Ecological Theology*, ed. Charles Birch, William Eakin, and Jay McDaniel (Maryknoll, NY: Orbis Books, 1990), 88–108. Classic statements of the women-earth connection are Rosemary Radford Ruether, *New Woman, New Earth* (San Francisco: Harper & Row, 1975); and Susan Griffin, *Woman and Nature: The Roaring Inside Her* (San Francisco: Harper & Row, 1978).

2. Rosemary Radford Ruether, *To Change the World: Christology and Cultural Criticism* (New York: Crossroad, 1981), 60. See the essays on the construction of gender in Anne Carr and Elisabeth Schüssler Fiorenza, eds., *The Special Nature of Women?* (Philadelphia: Trinity Press International, 1991), *Concilium* 6 (1991).

3. Heribert Mühlen, "The Person of the Holy Spirit," in *The Holy Spirit and Power*, ed. Kilian McDonnell (Garden City, NY: Doubleday, 1975), 12.

4. For fuller treatment of this point see Elizabeth Johnson, *She Who Is: The Mystery of God in Feminist Theological Discourse* (New York: Crossroad, 1992), 124–49.

5. For a remarkable new set of arguments in favor of emotional involvement on the part of medical practitioners, see Jodi Halpern, *From Detached Concern to Empathy: Humanizing Medical Practice* (Oxford: Oxford University Press, 2001). See also the constructive review of this book by Nancy R. Angoff, "Making a Place for Emotions in Medicine," *Yale Journal of Health Policy, Law, and Ethics* 2 (Spring 2002): 447–53.

6. See Margaret A. Farley, "How Shall We Love in a Postmodern World?," in *The Annual of the Society of Christian Ethics* (1994): 3–19.

7. This point has become almost a given in feminist theology. Valerie Saiving, "Human Experience: A Feminine View," *Journal of Religion* 40 (1960); for two representative examples, see Judith Plaskow, *Sex, Sin, and Grace: Women's Experience and the Theologies of Reinhold Niebuhr and Paul Tillich* (Washington, DC: University Press of America, 1980); Barbara Hilkert Andolsen, "Agape in Feminist Ethics," in *Feminist Theological Ethics: A Reader*, ed. Lois K. Daly (Louisville, KY: Westminster John Knox Press, 1994), 146–59.

8. See, for example, Edward C. Vacek, *Love, Human and Divine: The Heart of Christian Ethics* (Washington, DC: Georgetown University Press, 1994); Stephen Pope, *The Evolution of Altruism and the Ordering of Love* (Washington, DC: Georgetown University Press, 1994); Bernard V. Brady, *Christian Love* (Washington, DC: Georgetown University Press, 2003).

9. See, for example, Paula M. Cooey, Sharon A. Farmer, and Mary Ellen Ross, eds., *Embodied Love: Sensuality and Relationship as Feminist Values* (San Francisco: HarperSanFrancisco, 1987); Margaret Farley, *Personal Commitments: Beginning, Keeping, Changing* (San Francisco: HarperSanFrancisco, 1986), as well as Saiving, "Human Experience: A Feminine View"; Plaskow, *Sex, Sin, and Grace*; Andolsen, "Agape in Feminist Ethics," in *Feminist Theological Ethics*, 146–59.

10. Thomas Aquinas, *Summa Theologiae* II–II, q. 26, a. 4: "A man ought, out of charity, to love himself more than he loves any other person."

11. Elaine Scarry, *On Beauty and Being Just* (Princeton, NJ: Princeton University Press, 1999).

12. Scarry, *On Beauty and Being Just*, 23–24.

13. Scarry, *On Beauty and Being Just*, 29.

14. Frederick Turner, *Beauty: The Value of Values* (Charlottesville: University of Virginia Press, 1991), 2ff.

15. Turner, *Beauty*, 3; emphasis in the original.

16. David Bentley Hart, *The Beauty of the Infinite: The Aesthetics of Christian Truth* (Grand Rapids, MI: Eerdmans, 2003), 17–21.

17. Susan A. Ross, "Women, Beauty, and Justice: Moving Beyond von Balthasar," *Journal of the Society of Christian Ethics* 25, no. 1 (Spring/Summer 2005): 81.

18. Scarry, *On Beauty and Being Just*, 25.

19. The word *symbol* itself even seems to be suspect, as the recent silencing of Roger Haight, author of *Jesus Symbol of God* (Maryknoll, NY: Orbis Books, 1999), painfully illustrates.

20. Peter Russell, *From Science to God: A Physicist's Journey into the Mystery of Consciousness* (Novato, CA: New World Library, 2002), 63.

21. Russell, *From Science to God*, 64.

22. Russell, *From Science to God*, 64.

23. Russell, *From Science to God*, 56, citing Kant.

24. Russell, *From Science to God*, 42, citing Schrödinger.

25. Judith Plaskow, "Appropriation, Reciprocity, and Issues of Power," in *Feminist Theological Ethics: A Reader*, ed. Lois K. Daly (Louisville, KY: Westminster John Knox Press, 1994), 100.

26. Toinette M. Eugene, "On 'Difference' and the Dream of Pluralist Feminism," in Daly, *Feminist Theological Ethics*, 93.

27. Ada María Isasi-Díaz, "Viva la Diferencia!," in Daly, *Feminist Theological Ethics*, 95.

28. Mary Hunt, "Commentary," in Daly, *Feminist Theological Ethics*, 106.

29. Ellen M. Umansky, "Commentary," in Daly, *Feminist Theological Ethics*, 114.

30. Lawrence M. Wills, *Not God's People: Insiders and Outsiders in the Biblical World* (Lanham, MD: Rowman and Littlefield, 2008), 150–52.

31. Judith Plaskow, "Anti-Judaism in Feminist Christian Interpretation," in *Searching the Scriptures*, vol. 1, *A Feminist Introduction*, ed. Elisabeth Schüssler Fiorenza (New York: Crossroad, 1993), 119–22.

32. Plaskow, "Anti-Judaism in Feminist Christian Interpretation," 124–26.

33. Plaskow, "Anti-Judaism in Feminist Christian Interpretation," 127.

34. Paul Ricœur, *Essays on Biblical Interpretation*, ed. Lewis S. Mudge (Philadelphia: Fortress Press, 1980), 95; cited in Margaret Farley, "Feminist Consciousness and the Interpretation of Scripture," in *From Christ to the World: Introductory Readings in Christian Ethics*, ed. W. Boulton, T. Kennedy and A. Verhey (Grand Rapids, MI: Eerdmans, 1994), 52.

35. Riane Eisler uses this image in her own discussion of economy as *oikonomia*. Riane Eisler, *The Real Wealth of Nations: Creating a Caring Economics* (San Francisco: Berrett-Koehler, 2008), 12.

36. Wendell Berry, *Home Economics* (San Francisco: North Point Press, 1987), 54–75, esp. 54–58.

37. Martin Luther King, Jr., "The World House," in *Where Do We Go from Here? Chaos or Community?* (New York: Harper & Row, 1967), 177–202.

38. John A. Ryan, "Industrial Democracy," in *Better Economic Order* (New York: Harper, 1935), 148–74.

39. Joanna Moorhead, "Leonora Carrington Obituary," *The Guardian*, May 26, 2011, http://www.theguardian.com/artanddesign/2011/may/26/leonora-carrington-obituary.

40. Thomas Merton, *Thomas Merton: Selected Essays*, ed. Patrick F. O'Connell (Maryknoll, NY: Orbis Books, 2013), 6.

41. Merton, *Thomas Merton*, 7.

42. Bernard Lonergan, *Method in Theology* (Toronto: University of Toronto Press, 1971), 14–15.

43. Lonergan, *Method in Theology*, 35.

44. Lonergan, *Method in Theology*, 57.

45. Lonergan, *Method in Theology*, 238–44.

46. Stephen Bevans and Robert Schroeder, *Prophetic Dialogue: Reflection on Christian Mission Today* (Maryknoll, NY: Orbis Books, 2011), 21.

47. Lonergan, *Method in Theology*, 238.

48. James Fowler, *Stages of Faith: Psychology of Human Development and the Quest for Meaning* (New York: Harper Collins, 1995), 72–75, 78–79, 244.

49. Fowler, *Stages of Faith*, 30.

50. Lonergan, *Method in Theology*, 240.

51. JustFaith Ministries, http://justfaith.org/about-us/history-mission/.

52. Lonergan, *Method in Theology*, 240–41.

53. Thomas Aquinas, *Summa Theologiae*, II, II, q. 27, art 1, ad 2.

54. Lonergan, *Method in Theology*, 241.

55. C. G. Jung, *Psychology and Religion* (New York: Pantheon, 1958), 105.

56. John Dunne, *The Way of All the Earth* (New York: Macmillan, 1972), 221.

57. Donna Haraway, "Mice into Wormholes: A Comment on the Nature of No Nature," in *Cyborgs & Citadels: Anthropological Interventions in Emerging Sciences and Technologies*, ed. Gary Lee Downey and Joseph Dumit (Santa Fe, NM: School of American Research Press, 1998), 210.

58. Ann Kull, "Cyborg Embodiment and Incarnation," *Currents in Theology and Mission* 28, nos. 3–4 (2001): 283.

59. Kull, "Embodiment and Incarnation," 284.

60. Kull, "Embodiment and Incarnation," 284.

61. Gerd Theissen, *Biblical Faith: An Evolutionary Approach* (Minneapolis: Fortress Press, 1985), 112–13.

62. Theissen, *Biblical Faith*, 115.

63. Philip Hefner, "Theological Perspectives on Morality and Human Evolution," in *Religion and Science: History, Method, Dialogue*, ed. W. Mark Richardson and Wesley J. Wildman (New York: Routledge, 1996), 412.

64. Jim Marion, *Putting on the Mind of Christ: The Inner Work of Christian Spirituality* (Charlottesville, VA: Hampton Roads, 2000), 8.

65. Teilhard de Chardin, *Phenomenon of Man*, trans. Bernard Wall (New York: Harper and Row, 1959), 261.

Contributors

Mary C. Boys is the Skinner and McAlpin Professor of Practical Theology at Union Theological Seminary and its former academic vice president and dean. She has authored six books and numerous articles and has served as editor or coeditor of four books. Boys has received honorary doctorates from Hebrew Union College–Jewish Institute of Religion, Catholic Theological Union, Jewish Theological Seminary of America, Gratz College, and Misericordia University. She currently chairs the Committee on Ethics, Religion, and the Holocaust at the U.S. Holocaust Memorial Museum in Washington, DC. A Seattle native, she is a member of the Sisters of the Holy Names of Jesus and Mary.

Sidney Callahan earned her doctorate in clinical psychology from the City University of New York. In addition to being a licensed psychologist and tenured professor of psychology, Callahan is a public intellectual whose books, articles, and essays cover a range of issues in Catholic life, including bioethics, suffering, family, gender, and feminism. She also has served as a senior Distinguished Scholar at the Hastings Institute.

Denise Lardner Carmody (1935–2023) was a summa cum laude graduate of the College of Notre Dame in Maryland and earned a master's degree and doctorate in the philosophy of religion from Boston College. She was chair of the religious studies departments at both Wichita State University and the University of Tulsa prior to her arrival at Santa Clara University in 1994, where she spent the remainder of her career. She wrote more than sixty books on topics such as spirituality, world religions, feminist theology, and ethics, including several coauthored books with her husband, John Tully Carmody. They were the first married couple to win the Catholic Theological Society of America's distinguished John Courtney Murray Award.

Joan Chittister, OSB, is one of the most articulate social analysts and influential religious leaders of our time. A Benedictine Sister of Erie, Pennsylvania, Sister Joan is a national and international lecturer and award-winning author of sixty books on spirituality and peace and justice, especially for women in the church and society. A founding member of the Global Peace Initiative of Women, a partner organization of the United Nations, she has facilitated gatherings of spiritual leaders throughout the world. She served as president of the Leadership Conference of Women Religious, was prioress of her community for twelve years, and was an Elected Fellow/Von Hugel lecturer of St. Edmund's College, Cambridge University, England. In the 1991 spring semester, she served as Writer-in-Residence and commencement speaker at St. Mary's College.

Catherine E. Clifford is professor of systematic and historical theology at Saint Paul University, Ottawa. She continues to teach, lecture, and publish in the areas of ecclesiology, ecumenism, and the history of the Second Vatican Council. Since 2017, she has served as a member of the Methodist-Roman Catholic International Commission, and in 2023–2024 she was named as one of the first nonepiscopal delegates to the International Synod. Among her recent publications is *Vatican II at 60: Re-energizing the Renewal*, coedited with Stephen Lampe (Orbis, 2024) and *The Oxford Handbook on Vatican II*, coedited with Massimo Faggioli (Oxford University Press, 2023).

Mary Collins, OSB (1935–2024), earned a PhD in liturgical theology from Catholic University then taught religious studies at Benedictine College, the University of Kansas, and the Catholic University of America. She was elected prioress of Mount St. Scholastica Monastery in Atchison, Kansas, in 1999 and served as the first councilor for the Federation of St. Scholastica. She wrote, cowrote, or edited many articles and books, earning her honors from the National Association of Pastoral Musicians, the Notre Dame Center for Pastoral Liturgy, and the North American Academy of Liturgy.

M. Shawn Copeland is Professor Emerita of Systematic Theology at Boston College in Chestnut Hill, Massachusetts, and Theologian-in-Residence at Saint Katharine Drexel Parish in Roxbury, Massachusetts. She is the author, editor, or coeditor of eight books, including *Enfleshing Freedom: Body, Race, and Being* (2nd edition, 2023) and with Laurie Cassidy, *Desire, Darkness, and Hope: Theology in a Time of Impasse; Engaging the Thought of Constance FitzGerald, OCD*. Copeland is an internationally recognized, award-winning writer and scholar.

Ilia Delio, OSF, is a Franciscan Sister of Washington, DC and holds the Josephine C. Connelly Chair in Christian Theology at Villanova University. She is the author of over twenty-three books including *The Hours of the Universe: Reflections on God, Science and the Human Journey*, which won a 2022 Gold Nautilus Book Award; *Making All Things New: Catholicity, Cosmology and Consciousness*, a finalist for the 2019 Michael Ramsey Prize; and *The Unbearable Wholeness of Being: God, Evolution and the Power of Love*, for which she won the 2014 Silver Nautilus Book Award and a 2014 Catholic Press Association Book Award in Faith and Science. She is founder of the Center for Christogenesis, an online educational resource for promoting the vision of Teilhard de Chardin and, more broadly, the integration of science and religion in the twenty-first century.

Elizabeth Dreyer is Professor Emerita of Religious Studies at Fairfield University. She previously taught at the Catholic University of America; the Washington Theological Union in Washington, DC; and the College of St. Catherine in St. Paul, Minnesota. An expert in medieval women mystics, the history of Christian spirituality, and the role of women in Christianity, she is the author or coauthor of ten books. Dreyer is the recipient of the Elizabeth Ann Seton Medal from Mount Saint Joseph's College and Fairfield University's Choice Award for exemplary application of the ideals of the Ignatian tradition. She received her PhD from Marquette University.

Barbara Fiand, SNDdeN, taught spirituality at the Institute of Pastoral Studies of Loyola University Chicago and is the author of eleven books, including *From Religion Back to Faith: A Journey of the Heart*, *In the*

Stillness You Will Know: Exploring the Paths of Our Ancient Belonging, and *On Becoming Who We Are*. She lectures and gives retreats and workshops throughout the country and abroad on issues related to holistic spirituality, the transformation of consciousness, faith-seeking understanding in the twenty-first century, human maturation, and the true self.

Maria Harris (1932–2005) earned a joint EdD in education and religious studies from Columbia University's Teacher's College and Union Theological Seminary. She held a range of teaching and administrative positions in Catholic parochial schools, diocesan adult education, as well as Andover Newton Theological School and Fordham University's Graduate School of Religion and Religious Education. She wrote many books on religious education, parish ministry, teaching, spirituality, and feminism, including two she coauthored with her husband Gabriel Moran.

Monika K. Hellwig (1929–2005) migrated from Germany to the United States as a young girl during World War II and then went on to become a distinguished leader in twentieth-century American Catholicism. After receiving her doctorate from Catholic University of America, she taught for more than three decades at Georgetown University. Hellwig served as president and executive director of the Association of Catholic Colleges and as president of the Catholic Theological Society of America. For her leadership and scholarship, which included two dozen books, Hellwig received thirty-two honorary degrees and fifteen named awards, including the John Courtney Murray Award, the highest honor bestowed by the Catholic Theological Society of America.

Mary Catherine Hilkert, a member of the Dominican Sisters of Peace, is professor of systematic theology at the University of Notre Dame. She is the author of *Naming Grace: Preaching and the Sacramental Imagination*, *Speaking with Authority: Catherine of Siena and the Voices of Women Today*, and *A Time to Keep Silence and a Time to Speak* and is a regular contributor to scholarly and pastoral journals in the areas of contemporary theology, preaching, and spirituality.

Mary Ann Hinsdale, IHM, is Professor Emerita in the Theology Department at Boston College, where she taught from 2000 to 2024. She holds a PhD in systematic theology from the University of St. Michael's (Toronto) and specializes in theological anthropology, ecological theologies, ecclesiology, and intercultural feminist theologies. She also taught at the College of the Holy Cross in Worcester, MA (1987–2000), where she chaired the Department of Religious Studies and directed the Women's Studies Program, and at St. John's Provincial Seminary, Plymouth, MI (1982–1987). She is coeditor and contributor to the *T&T Clark's Companion to Theological Anthropology* (Bloomsbury, 2021). A former president of the Catholic Theological Society of America, she received the Elizabeth Ann Seton Award (2017) and the Yves Congar Award (2024), both for theological excellence.

Christine Firer Hinze is professor of theological and social ethics at Fordham University, New York. Her teaching and research focus on foundational and applied issues in Christian social ethics with special emphasis on the dynamics of power and social transformation, Catholic social thought, and economic and work justice for vulnerable women, families, and groups. Her most recent book is *Radical Sufficiency: Work, Livelihood and a U.S. Catholic Economic Ethic* (Georgetown University Press, 2021).

Kathleen Hughes, RSCJ, is a sacramental theologian, teacher, speaker, and writer. For nineteen years, Hughes was professor of word and worship at Catholic Theological Union in Chicago. She left CTU to become provincial of her religious order, the Society of the Sacred Heart in the United States, and led her order for six years. She is now occupied with issues of spirituality and prayer and the retrieval and reinterpretation of traditional wisdom and practice for contemporary life.

Elizabeth Johnson, CSJ, is Distinguished Professor Emerita at Fordham University in New York City. Former president of the Catholic Theological Society of America and also of the ecumenical American Theological Society, she loves to teach, mentor, research, and write. Recipient of fifteen honorary doctorates and numerous other awards, she has developed themes of her Madeleva Lecture in later books such as *Ask the Beasts* (2014), *Creation and the Cross* (2018), and *Come, Have Breakfast* (2024).

Kwok Pui-lan is William F. Cole Professor of Christian Theology and Spirituality Emerita at Episcopal Divinity School and a past president of the American Academy of Religion. She has published extensively in Asian and Asian American feminist theology, biblical interpretation, and postcolonial criticism. An internationally known theologian, Kwok's recent publications include *The Anglican Tradition from a Postcolonial Perspective* (Church Publishing, 2023) and *Postcolonial Politics and Theology* (Westminster John Knox, 2021).

Dolores Leckey (1933–2023) was founding director of the U.S. bishops' Secretariat for the Laity, where she served for two decades before working as a senior fellow at Woodstock Theological Center at Georgetown University. A celebrated retreat speaker and spiritual writer, she published more than a dozen books on lay spirituality and ministry and was the recipient of thirteen honorary degrees and the St. Elizabeth Seton Medal from Mount St. Joseph University in Cincinnati.

Gail Porter Mandell is Professor and Schlesinger Endowed Chair Emerita of the Humanistic Studies Program at Saint Mary's College, Notre Dame, Indiana. She holds a PhD in English from the University of Notre Dame. Her publications include *Angel Creek, Where the River Meets the Sea: A Memoir* (University of the West Indies Press, 2014), *Madeleva: A Biography* (SUNY Press, 1997), and *Life into Art: Conversations with Seven Contemporary Biographers* (University of Arkansas Press, 1991).

Kathleen Norris is the author of *Journey: New and Selected Poems*, *Dakota: A Spiritual Geography*, *The Cloister Walk*, *Acedia and Me*, and *A Whole Life in 12 Movies*. She writes regularly for *Give Us This Day* and an e-newsletter, "Soul Telegram: Movies & Meaning." A graduate of Bennington College, she has been a Benedictine oblate since 1987 and has taught at Providence College, the Collegeville Institute, and the School of Theology at St. John's University in Minnesota.

Mercy Amba Oduyoye is the first woman in Africa to obtain a university degree in theology and with this training, has taught in several universities in Africa and in the United States. Oduyoye served major ecumenical organizations including the All-African Council of Churches and the World Council of Churches, where she ended up as deputy general secretary. In 1989, Oduyoye initiated the Circle of Concerned African Women Theologians, which has mentored many women in the theological field and has produced at least 150 books and more than 1000 articles. Oduyoye has authored five books and numerous articles and edited four anthologies. She is the recipient of numerous awards and honorary doctorates.

Anne Patrick, SNJM (1941–2016), earned her PhD in religion and literature at the University of Chicago, where she taught at the Divinity School before joining the faculty at Carleton College. A scholar of moral theology, she held leadership positions in the Society of Christian Ethics and the International Network of Societies of Catholic Theology. Patrick also served as president of the Catholic Theological Society of America, which also gave her the Ann O'Hara Graff Award from the Women's Consultation in Constructive Theology and the John Courtney Murray Award, the society's highest recognition.

Nancy Pineda-Madrid holds the T. Marie Chilton Chair of Catholic Theology at Loyola Marymount University. She published the first book to offer a theological interpretation of the tragic killing of women because they are women (feminicide), that is, *Suffering and Salvation in Ciudad Juárez* (Fortress, 2011). Her current book project offers a Latina feminist reading of the theological symbol of Our Lady of Guadalupe. She is president of the Catholic Theological Society of America (2024–2025).

Jeanette Rodriguez is professor at Seattle University in the Department of Theology and Religious Studies. She serves as executive director of the Institute for Catholic Thought and Culture, holds the Malcolm and Mari Stamper Endowed Chair in Catholic Intellectual and Cultural Traditions, and cochairs the *Laudato Si'* Action Platform Steering Committee. Rodriguez is the author of several books and articles concentrated in the areas of U.S. Hispanic theology, theologies of liberation, peacebuilding, and women's spirituality, including *Our Lady of Guadalupe: Faith and Empowerment among Mexican American Women* (1994); *Stories We Live* (1996); coeditor with Maria Pilar Aquino and Daisy Machado of *A Reader in Latina Feminist Theology* (2002); coauthor with Ted Fortier of *Cultural Memory: Resistance, Faith and Identity* (2007); *A Clan Mother's Call* (2017), and most recently coauthor with Sharon Callahan of *Women Called to Catholic Priesthood: From Ecclesial Challenge to Spiritual Renewal* (2024).

Sandra M. Schneiders was born in Chicago, Illinois, in 1936 and made Religious Profession as an IHM Sister in Monroe, Michigan, in 1958. She received her BA in sociology from Marygrove College in Detroit, Michigan; an MA in philosophy from the University of Detroit; the STL from the Institut Catholique in Paris; and the STD in New Testament and spirituality from the Gregorian University in Rome. She is the author of fifteen books and more than a hundred articles. She is Professor Emerita of the Jesuit School of Theology of Santa Clara University, where she taught from 1976 to 2020 and currently lives and works in Monroe, Michigan.

Wendy M. Wright is Emerita Professor of Theology at Creighton University and affiliate faculty at Oblate School of Theology Institute for Study of Contemporary Spirituality. Wright is the author of seventeen books, the most recent of which is the coedited *The Nineteenth Century Salesian Pentecost* in the Paulist Press Classics of Western Spirituality series (2022). She has written over sixty academic articles in books, refereed journals, and monographs with another eighty plus articles published in pastoral publications.